Springer Series on Medical Education

SERIES EDITOR: Steven Jonas, M.D.

VOLUME 1 Problem-Based Learning: An Approach to Medical Education
Howard S. Barrows, M.D., and Robyn M. Tamblyn, B.Sc.N.

VOLUME 2 The Evaluation of Teaching in Medical Schools
Robert M. Rippey, Ph.D.

VOLUME 3 The Art of Teaching Primary Care
Archie S. Golden, M.D., M.P.H., Dennis G. Carlson, M.D., M.P.H., M.A., and Jan L. Hagen, M.S.W., *Editors*

VOLUME 4 Medical Education in the Ambulatory Setting: An Evaluation
Loyd J. Wollstadt, M.D., Sc.M., Dennis A. Frate, Ph.D., and Mark G. Meyer, M.A.T.

VOLUME 5 Teaching Preventive Medicine in Primary Care
William H. Barker, M.D.

VOLUME 6 The Interpersonal Dimension in Medical Education
Agnes G. Rezler, Ph.D., and Joseph A. Flaherty, M.D.

VOLUME 7 Assessing Clinical Competence
Victor R. Neufeld, M.D., FRCP (C), and Geoffrey R. Norman, Ph.D., *Editors*

VOLUME 8 How to Design a Problem-Based Curriculum for the Preclinical Years
Howard S. Barrows, M.D., FRCP (C)

VOLUME 9 Implementing Problem-Besed Medical Education: Lessons from Successful Innovations
Arthur Kaufman, M.D., *Editor*

VOLUME 10 Clinical Teaching for Medical Residents: Roles, Techniques, and Programs
Janine C. Edwards, Ph.D., and Robert L. Marier, M.D., FACP, *Editors*

VOLUME 11 A Practical Guide to Clinical Teaching in Medicine
Kaaren C. Douglas, M.D., M.S.P.H., Michael C. Hosokawa, Ed.D., and Frank H. Lawler, M.D., M.S.P.H.

VOLUME 12 Successful Faculty in Academic Medicine: Essential Skills and How to Acquire Them
Carole J. Bland, Ph.D., Constance C. Schmitz, M.A., Frank T. Stritter, Ph.D., Rebecca C. Henry, Ph.D., and John J. Aluise, Ph.D.

VOLUME 13 Innovation in Medical Education: An Evaluation of Its Present Status
Zohair M. Nooman, Henk G. Schmidt, and Esmat S. Ezzat, *Editors*

VOLUME 14 The Politics of Reform in Medical Education and Health Services: The Negev Project
Basil Porter, M.B.B.Ch., M.P.H., and William E. Seidelman, M.D.

VOLUME 15 Medical Teaching in Ambulatory Care: A Practical Guide
Warren Rubenstein, M.D., and Yves Talbot, M.D.

VOLUME 16 Collaborative Clinical Education: The Foundation of Effective Health Care
Jane Westberg, Ph.D., and Hilliard Jason, M.D.

VOLUME 17 Assessment Measures in Medical School, Residency, and Practice: The Connections
Joseph S. Gonnella, M.D., Mohammadreza Hojat, Ph.D., James B. Erdmann, Ph.D., and J. Jon Veloski, M.S.

VOLUME 18 Teaching Creatively with Video: Fostering Reflection, Communication and Other Clinical Skills
Jane Westberg, Ph.D., and Hilliard Jason, M.D.

Jane Westberg, Ph.D., has devoted more than 20 years helping to improve the quality of health care by working to enhance the quality of teaching in the health professions. She has served on the faculties of the University of Miami School of Medicine and the George Washington University School of Medicine. Currently, she is Associate Clinical Professor in the Department of Family Medicine at the University of Colorado School of Medicine and Director of the Center for Instructional Support in Boulder, Colorado. She has designed and run workshops for thousands of health professions educators and has served as a consultant to health professions education programs throughout the United States and in several other countries. Throughout her career, she has used video extensively in her teaching of students, residents, and faculty members. She was lead writer and producer for three video series (*Clinical Teaching, Communicating with Patients*, and *Relating Effectively to Surgical Patients*); a 24-program series broadcast on the Hospital Satellite Network (*Pediatric Horizons*); and *Making Effective Presentations*. She is first author of *Collaborative Clinical Education: The Foundation of Effective Patient Care* (Springer Publishing Company) and has written numerous articles, chapters, instructional materials, and other books for health professions educators.

Hilliard Jason, M.D., Ed.D., has devoted his career since the late 1950s to finding ways to enhance the quality of teaching in the health professions. He was founding Director of the Office of Medical Education (OMERAD) at Michigan State University's College of Human Medicine, the Division of Faculty Development at the Association of American Medical Colleges (AAMC), and the National Center for Faculty Development at the University of Miami School of Medicine. He is now Executive Director of the Center for Instructional Support in Boulder, Colorado and Clinical Professor of Family Medicine at the University of Colorado School of Medicine. He has been a consultant to most of the medical schools in the United States and Canada and has run workshops for health professions teachers in 19 countries. He is the senior author of *Teachers and Teaching in U.S. Medical Schools* and has written extensively in the areas of faculty development and medical teaching. He helped pioneer the use of video, video triggers, and simulated patients in medical teaching and has been the executive producer, writer, and host of more than 50 educational video programs, including a program for the public on patients' rights for PBS; a 24-part series for child health professionals broadcast on HSN; a 7-part series on teaching interpersonal skills produced at WGBH, Boston; and several series on aspects of effective teaching and effective communication that are used in medical and nursing education programs internationally.

TEACHING CREATIVELY WITH VIDEO

Fostering Reflection, Communication and Other Clinical Skills

Jane Westberg, PhD
Hilliard Jason, MD, EdD

SPRINGER PUBLISHING COMPANY
New York

Springer Publishing Company, Inc.
536 Broadway
New York, NY 10012

94 95 96 97 98 / 5 4 3 2 1

Library of Congress Catloging-in-Publication Data

Westberg, Jane
Teaching creatively with video : fostering reflection, communication and other clinical skills
/ Jane Westberg, Hilliard Jason.
p. cm.
Includes bibliographical references and indexes.
ISBN 0-8261-8360-3
1. Health education—Audio-visual aids. 2. Video recordings.
3. Medicine--Study and teaching—Audio-visual aids. I. Jason, Hilliard, 1933– . II. Title
RA440.55.W47 1994
613' . 078—dc20 93-4377
CIP

Printed in the United States of America

Contents

List of Appendices vii

Introduction ix

1. Managing Instructional Challenges 3

Part I: Using Video in the Classroom 25

2. Using Video for Illustrating, Modeling, and Demonstrating 27

3. Selecting and Using Video Triggers 55

4. Making and Reviewing Tapes of Role-Played Exercises 83

Part II: Using Video in Clinical Supervision 109

5. Preparing for and Making Recordings 111

6. Helping Learners Use Video for Reflection and Self-Assessment 131

7. Using Video for Providing Constructive Feedback 161

8. Helping Learners Use Video for Peer Review 179

9. Eliciting Patients' Perspectives 199

Epilogue 219

Glossary 221

References 227

Author Index 233

Subject Index 235

Contents

List of Appendices

2.1 Self-Checklist: Preparing for a Videotaped Demonstration 53

2.2 Self-Checklist: Reviewing a Video Recording with Learners 54

3.1 Some Sources of Video Triggers in the Health Professions 79

3.2 Self-Checklist: Preparing to Use Video Clips 80

3.3 Self-Checklist: Using Video Triggers 81

4.1 Self-Checklist: Preparing Learners for and Doing the Initial Videotaped Role Play 107

4.2 Self-Checklist: Reviewing the Recording 108

5.1 Self-Checklist: Preparing for Making Recordings 129

5.2 Self-Checklist: Making Recordings 130

6.1 Self-Checklist for Educators: Using Video for Guiding Learner Self-Assessments 157

6.2 Self-Checklist for Health Professionals: Opening of Interview 159

7.1 Self-Checklist for Educators: Giving Feedback to Learners 176

7.2 Evaluation Form for Educators: Opening of Interview 177

8.1 Self-Checklist for Peers: Giving Feedback to Peers 195

8.2 Evaluation Form for Peers: Opening of Interview 196

8.3 Self-Checklist: Preparing Learners for Peer Review Using Video 197

8.4 Self-Checklist for Educators: Facilitating Peer Review Using Video 198

9.1 Evaluation of Care: Patient's Form 214

9.2 Evaluation of Care: Provider's Form 215

9.3 Evaluation of Care: Peer's Form 216

9.4 Self-Check List for Educators: Reviewing Video Recordings with Learners and Patients 217

Introduction

This book is intended for educators who recognize that many of our conventional instructional practices are inadequate for the considerable challenges we face when seeking to prepare people to be effective health professionals and devoted lifelong learners. The information and recommendations in this book are likely to be of most interest to those who are looking for creative solutions to the instructional challenges they face when teaching in classrooms, conference rooms, and patient care settings. Although we focus on educating health professionals, the principles and most of the strategies we discuss also apply to educating other professionals (e.g., lawyers, college and university professors, and teachers in elementary and secondary schools).

THE AREAS OF FOCUS

Educating health professionals is a tough job. Far more is required than merely conveying information. Helping people gain the array of skills and attitudes required for sustained high standards and exemplary performance demands that we provide a set of appropriate conditions. Explicit circumstances are needed to foster the learning of habits and capabilities that form the foundation of successful professional work.

In Chapter 1 we emphasize the conditions that educational programs must provide if students and residents are to achieve lasting learning. We also present a collaborative model for teaching and learning that we argue is needed for learners to derive as much as possible from their formal education and to become professionals who provide high-quality care to those they serve. Achieving these challenging goals requires considerable skill from us and the effective use of whatever resources can contribute to this process. The most potent of all currently available instructional resources, in our view, is properly and creatively used video. In the first chapter we summarize some of the ways that you can use video for providing learners with the conditions and opportunities they need. And we indicate how video is particularly well suited for teaching and learning the *processes* of health care (e.g., *how* we interact with patients and colleagues, how we identify and think through health care problems).

In Chapters 2–4 we focus on ways you can use video to make classrooms and conference rooms arenas of active, significant learning. Video can help convert typically passive experiences into ones in which learners are actively engaged in doing intellectual and other tasks that are vital to their becoming competent providers of health care. We explain ways you can shape the learning environment and be a "producer" of instructional events that give learners the challenges they need. In Chapter 2 we discuss ways to use video programs and video clips to illustrate the health care challenges that learners need to be prepared to face and manage. We also explore making and using recordings of yourself so that you can serve as a role model and clearly demonstrate the capabilities learners will need when providing health care. In Chapter 3 we discuss ways to use video triggers (brief video clips) to provoke reflection, stimulate lively discussions, enable learners to practice dealing with tough emotional and intellectual challenges, and more. In Chapter 4 we discuss how role playing can help both beginning and advanced learners practice and refine their clinical skills. We also explore how making and reviewing tapes of role plays can enrich role-playing experiences and prepare learners to be reflective about and good assessors of the care they provide to patients.

Chapters 5–9 deal with using video in supervising learners as they care for patients/clients in health care centers, hospitals, and other settings. In Chapter 5 we discuss the details and challenges involved in making video recordings of your learners as they interact with patients or carry out other tasks. Then we explore ways to use these recordings to help learners reflect on and assess their work (Chapter 6), to provide learners with your constructive feedback (Chapter 7), to engage learners in reviewing and learning from each other's experiences (Chapter 8), and to elicit patients' feedback (Chapter 9).

This is not a technical book on the mechanics of video. Unlike the many technical books available on video, we focus primarily on the human issues involved when making and using video recordings in health professions education (e.g., how to prepare learners for being videotaped and for reviewing recordings of their work, how to secure patients' informed consent and prepare them for being videotaped, how to be minimally disruptive when videotaping in a busy health care setting). We also provide enough basic information on creating and presenting videos that you should be able to proceed with any of our recommended instructional strategies, if you choose, without needing additional technical references.

THE ORGANIZATION OF THE BOOK

The book is organized for easy use. In the first part of each of Chapters 2–9 we present the rationale for using video for various tasks, such as providing constructive feedback, and the issues and considerations involved in carrying out the instructional strategies recommended in that chapter. These chapters all end with a "Suggestions" section in which we provide practical, step-by-step recommendations for using the strategy described in the first part of the chapter. The suggestions can serve several purposes, depending on your preferred use of this book. Readers who do not want to linger with the rationale and background provided in the earlier part of each chapter can go directly to the suggestions. For those who read the earlier parts of each chapter, the suggestions can provide a consolidation and summary, as well as concrete specifics, deriving from the reasons and explanations presented earlier. After your first pass through this book, the suggestions in each chapter can also provide quick reminders of specific strategies and techniques.

The suggestions are not cookbook-type recipes for effective teaching. Effective teaching and learning cannot be reduced to precise steps and exact ingredients. Rather—continuing with the cooking metaphor—we recommend some ingredients to consider and even the sequence for using those ingredients. Each teaching-learning encounter, however, is unique. Creative teaching, like creative cooking, requires improvisation and artistry, sometimes even inventing elements of the process as you go along.

At the end of most chapters are one or more appendixes, most of which present checklists that summarize the suggestions provided in that chapter. These checklists are meant as memory joggers and resources in support of your day-to-day teaching. Owners of this book have permission to photocopy these checklists for personal use.

THE LANGUAGE USED IN THE BOOK

In an attempt to speak to a range of educators, we use inclusive, generic terms, a few of which we have redefined. *Learners* include undergraduate students, graduate students, postgraduate students (including residents and house officers), fellows, and in some cases, health professionals who are participating in continuing education programs. *Health professionals, practitioners,* and *clinicians* are used interchangeably and include all professionals who provide health and medical care, including mental health care. *Clinical skills* are those skills that health professionals use in caring for people. Clinical learning experiences (CLEs) are the preceptorships, clerkships, rotations, practicums, and courses that provide learners with supervised patient care experiences.

Most often we refer to people who are seeking and receiving health care as *patients*, but in most instances the term *clients* may be substituted. We know that some people consider the term *patient* to be associated with an authoritarian form of care in which people are encouraged to function more as passive recipients of care than as partners in their care. As we discuss later, we advocate a collaborative model in both health care and education. In collaborative health care people are encouraged and helped to be as active in their care as possible, to be genuine partners in the process of their care. In collaborative education, students are encouraged to be active participants in their learning.

To deal with the issue of gender and avoid such awkward constructions as "herself/himself" and "his/hers," we use the plural whenever possible. Otherwise we try to alternate the use of male and female pronouns.

Video terms are italicized and defined when they first appear in the text. A glossary of video terms is found at the end of the book.

THE RAPIDLY CHANGING WORLD OF VIDEO

The technical side of video is in a state of perpetual evolution. Any intellectual material that is fixed in time, as is the information in books, is at risk of seeming out of date by the time it is read. In response to this inescapable condition, we have tried to focus more on general principles than on specific technologies. Still, some readers will notice our neglect of the rapidly emerging areas of *digital video*, *interactive video*, and *desktop video*. As of this writing, these developments are not yet in general use in health professions schools and do not yet have direct relevance to the day-to-day work of most of our intended readers; therefore we are deferring a full examination of these topics until a later writing.

AN APPRECIATION

This book is the product of the direct and indirect contributions of far more people than we can acknowledge here. They include the many teachers, residents, and students with whom we have been privileged to work. We give special thanks to Norman Kagan, whose use of film and video in the teaching of mental health professionals and others since the 1960s contributed substantially to our thinking about the uses of video in teaching the processes of health care. We are especially grateful to those who reviewed and critiqued a preliminary version of this work. Their comments and recommendations are reflected in whatever you find worthy in this book. They were Wayne Bottom, PA-C, Director, Physician Assistant Program, University of Florida; J. Gregory Carroll, Ph.D., Director, Miles Institute for Health Care Communication; Don Heider, University of Colorado at Boulder, School of Journalism and Mass Communications; Norman Kagan, Ph.D., Director, Interpersonal Process Recall Institute, University of Houston; Charles Lewis, M.D., Professor of Medicine, University of California at Los Angeles; Michael Magill, M.D., Senior Vice President for Medical Education and Outreach, Tallahassee Memorial Medical Center; Kathleen Mikan, R.N., Ph.D., Professor, School of Nursing, University of Alabama at Birmingham; and Carolyn Robinowitz, M.D., Senior Deputy Medical Director, American Psychiatric Association.

Jane Westberg, Ph.D. and Hilliard Jason, M.D., Ed.D.
Boulder, Colorado

1

Teaching Creatively with Video

CHAPTER 1

Managing Instructional Challenges

Helping learners become physicians, nurses, or other health professionals who routinely provide sensitive, competent care is a substantial challenge. Ensuring that our learners develop the capabilities they need to continue growing as professionals throughout their careers is an additional major challenge.

Successfully helping our students and residents develop the capabilities they need requires that we provide them with the following *conditions needed for lasting learning*:

- an understanding of the challenges and tasks they will face in their future work
- clarity about the capabilities they must develop to meet those challenges and tasks
- opportunities for staged, supervised practice of these capabilities
- opportunities to reflect on and assess their performance
- constructive feedback on their efforts
- trust-based relationships with us and their peers.

If they are to become and remain effective lifelong learners, our students and residents need to be active partners in planning, implementing, and monitoring their education. Our ways of interacting with them need to be collaborative, not authoritarian. And to support them in their learning, we need access to how they think and feel and what they do when faced with real health care challenges.

Too often, classrooms are dull places for learners and teachers. During many lectures, students doodle, daydream, sleep, or prepare for exams. Even when they are attentive, they usually can't concentrate on what is being said for more than 15 minutes at a time. When lecturing is a dominant instructional strategy, learners forget as much as 50% of course content within two months (Cross, 1986).

Can those of us who teach in classrooms actively engage our learners? How can we help them see that the topics we address are relevant to their future work? How can we give them opportunities to practice new skills and reflect on their performance?

Those of us who supervise students and residents in health care settings do not usually have a problem helping learners understand how their learning experiences are relevant to their future work (although this connection is not always automatic). If there are sufficient numbers of patients, there are usually opportunities for the learners to practice new capabilities. But, contrary to the widely cited aphorism, practice does not always make perfect, and we can't always be available to assure that our learners have the staged, supervised practice they need. Also, although providing constructive feedback is one of our most important instructional tasks, few of us have had systematic preparation for exercising this skill. Finally, our feedback should be based, at least in part, on our directly observing our learners as they engage in patient care tasks. But doing so is seldom easy.

No single technique or technology can be the magic solution for this array of instructional challenges. Yet video, when used creatively and constructively, can be a powerful tool for helping provide learners with the conditions they need for lasting learning. Video enables us to illustrate, model, and demonstrate events and strategies that are central to effective health care. It can present and clarify for learners the challenges they will face and the capabilities they need to develop. Also, video is especially well suited for teaching the interpersonal and cognitive *processes* that are central to functioning effectively as a provider of health care. (Building trust-based relationships, eliciting sensitive information from patients and their families, and providing advice or bad news are examples of interpersonal processes. Recognizing, assessing, and solving problems are examples of cognitive processes.)

In this chapter, we discuss the following:

- the conditions needed for lasting learning
- the collaborative model of education
- information teachers need for facilitating their students' learning
- the video resources and equipment that we will focus on in this book
- key elements of teaching in the classroom and in health care settings
- how video can help us provide the conditions needed for lasting learning when teaching in classrooms and when supervising learners in health care settings
- issues and considerations to keep in mind when using video in educating health professionals.

CONDITIONS NEEDED FOR LASTING LEARNING

A premise of this book is that being educators implies that we are capable of providing our students and residents with the conditions they need for lasting learning. (Note: The conditions for lasting learning that we propose here differ from those described by Gagne [1965].) Before exploring how video can help us provide the conditions needed for lasting learning, we describe and discuss the conditions themselves.

An Understanding of the Challenges and Tasks They Will Face in Their Future Work

By the time that students are enrolled in schools in the health professions, they are usually well adapted to the tasks of academe, so they accept the need for listening to lectures on topics that seem unrelated to their future work, and they obediently memorize material for exams they abhor but know they must pass if they are to reach their distant goal. Practicing the tasks of acquiescing to poorly understood or disagreeable demands is hardly optimal preparation for a life of independent, persistent learning. One doesn't learn to be free in jail, and one doesn't learn to be an independent learner in an atmosphere of prescribed, unwelcome assignments. If we are to help learners feel a sense of ownership of their own learning, internalize and sustain what they learn, and take initiative in their continuing learning, we need to find ways of assuring that they are aware of the health care needs of people and that they understand how what they are learning equips them for responding effectively to these needs.

Clarity about the Capabilities They Need for Their Future Work

If students and residents are to work hard at developing the capabilities they require as professionals, they need a clear picture of what they are working toward. They need to see people modeling these capabilities, and they need access to the *invisible processes* of health care—what their role models are thinking and feeling while providing care.

Opportunities for Systematic, Sequenced, Supervised Practice of Needed Capabilities

The act of providing health care can be seen as a performing art. It involves a good deal of personal latitude in shaping the many variables and skills that determine the ultimate impact one has on those being served. So, as in other performing arts, learners need opportunities for practicing the processes of health care. If our learners are to become reliably competent at doing their various patient care tasks, they must use the needed skills repeatedly. However, the unsupervised or minimally supervised trial-and-error approach to practice that characterizes much of clinical education can be inefficient, can lead to the solidification of bad habits, and can be hurtful to patients and learners.

Although practice is vital for acquiring, assimilating, and refining new skills, these new skills are learned effectively, efficiently, safely, and dependably only if the learners' practice is systematic, sequenced, and supervised. Practice needs to be carefully planned so that it is adapted to the learners' evolving levels of ability and readiness. As learners gain proficiency, they need higher levels of challenge. And skilled teachers need to oversee the process, as we discuss below, guiding learners in their self-assessments of their work and providing them with feedback based on their practice.

Opportunities to Reflect on and Assess Their Work

Learners may have numerous potentially valuable experiences, but much of this potential can be lost if they don't stop to reflect on and review these experiences. Too many health professions learners have such busy days and weeks that later, in retrospect, they can barely remember what they did, let alone extract the maximum learning potential from each experience. While interacting with patients, learners might be prompted to consider an intriguing issue but then have to move on to the next patient and the next patient, until the seedling idea is gone from their awareness. Each patient interaction can be a source of learning, but if learners fill every minute with pressured activity and do not pause to review their patient encounters or their other clinical experiences, potentially valuable lessons can be lost. Chickering (1977) argued that activities that are not checked by observation and analysis may be enjoyable, but intellectually they usually lead nowhere, neither to greater clarification nor to new ideas. To create a lasting record of the significant elements of an experience, learners need to be critically reflective.

In the world of sports, when coaches routinely videotape athletes engaged in their sport and then review the recordings with the athletes, they are acknowledging the importance of reviewing and reflecting on performance. Rather than having athletes spend all of their time practicing, these coaches have learned that athletes need to interrupt their practice to learn from what they have been doing.

Being reflective and constructively self-critical is essential if our students and residents are to help direct their learning while they are in our school or program. Having the capacity to accurately assess their strengths and areas of need and being able to formulate learning goals and plans based on their needs and interests is critical if they are to continue growing as professionals.

Brookfield (1986) described the cyclic nature of learning when he discussed the need for educational activity "to engage the learner in a continuous and alternating process of investigation and exploration, followed by action grounded in this exploration, followed by reflection on this action, followed by further investigation and exploration, followed by further action, and so on" (p. 15).

Constructive Feedback on Their Efforts

Feedback is fundamental to learning. Imagine trying to learn to steer a sailboat on a straight course in a situation where you do not get any information on the consequences of your actions. If you wore a blindfold when trying to steer the boat and received no verbal feedback, you would not know whether you were headed in the right direction or going wildly off course. Without that feedback, you would not know what adjustments to make to sustain or return to your course. Or think of someone who has no knowledge of piano trying to learn to play a tune while wearing ear plugs that prevent him from hearing the sounds he is producing. This would be an impossible task.

Our learners also need specific, accurate feedback on their performance, including what they are doing well and what they need to work on. If they receive such feedback in a timely way, their learning is likely to be accelerated.

Without feedback, our learners' mistakes can go uncorrected, and they can develop and solidify bad habits. Conversely, if they don't receive feedback on their strengths, they are at risk for discontinuing some of their desirable behaviors. Learners who have instinctive skills as systematic problem solvers, who are inherently sensitive to patients' concerns, or who have an effectively open-ended approach to interviewing may not necessarily know they have these capabilities or that these attributes are valued unless we give them feedback.

The minimal amounts of helpful feedback that some learners receive can cause them to be on a continuing lookout for clues from their supervisors. When explicit feedback is not forthcoming, learners are inclined to fill the vacuum with whatever crumbs are available and with their own assumptions, neither of which is usually helpful to learning.

Withholding or failing to offer helpful feedback to learners does not necessarily provide them with a neutral experience. For example a student who observes that her supervisor looks discouraged and unhappy may conclude that the supervisor is dissatisfied with her performance, although the supervisor may look that way because of a patient's unexpected setback. He may indeed be satisfied with the student's efforts.

When needed or expected feedback is missing, some learners conclude they are not doing well, even though they may be. Other learners assume they are doing well when in fact their performance is inadequate. Both groups are badly served by teachers who do not provide sufficient feedback.

Learners need feedback from us and their other teachers, but, as we discuss later, they can also benefit from feedback from their peers (other learners), patients, and staff.

A Trust-based Relationship with Us and Their Peers

Meaningful learning requires taking risks. On their way to developing complex capabilities, learners need to be open with themselves and with us about their strengths and deficiencies, and they need to be willing to go through the awkward, clumsy periods that inevitably accompany significant new learning. If learners are to take such risks, they need to feel confident that we will not use anything that they have revealed to us to hurt them. They also need to feel confident that our suggestions and advice are worthy.

If teaching and learning are to occur jointly with other learners, these peers also need to trust each other. The more they need to take risks in the presence of their peers, the higher their level of trust must be.

THE COLLABORATIVE MODEL

Becoming and remaining an effective health professional is a never-ending process. Knowledge in the sciences basic to health care and in the clinical disciplines is growing and changing continuously, and neither the art nor the science of providing health care is ever fully mastered. If our learners are to get the most out of their formal education and to continue growing throughout their careers, they need to acquire the skills and commitments involved in being competent, self-directed learners while they are still with us; they are unlikely to develop these capabilities spontaneously later. Logical analysis and available evidence support the premise that these instructional goals are more likely to be achieved using a *collaborative*—rather than the more traditional *authoritarian*—approach. Most of the suggestions in this book for ways to use video effectively in educating health professionals are based on the collaborative model.

The ways that learners and teachers interact range from collaborative to authoritarian. At the collaborative end of the continuum, students are active participants in their learning. At the authoritarian end of the continuum, learners are recipients of decisions and actions taken by others. Most instruction in the health professions falls between the extremes but is closer to the authoritarian end of the continuum. The contrasting characteristics of collaborative and authoritarian teacher-learner and learner-learner relationships are summarized in Table 1.1.

Collaborative education recognizes that the acquisition and application of knowledge are fundamentally social acts. Learners are helped to be self-directed while also being encouraged to work with each other, establishing mutual goals, working out ways they can help each other reach these goals, and providing helpful

TABLE 1.1 Contrasting Characteristics of Collaborative and Authoritarian Teacher-Learner Relationships

Collaborative	*Authoritarian*
Learners are treated as valuable contributors to their own and to each other's learning.	Learners are treated primarily as recipients of teaching.
The teacher and learners jointly set the agenda.	The teacher sets the agenda.
Learners participate in assessing their learning needs.	The teacher presumes to know the learners' learning needs.
The teacher and learners establish individual and shared goals of learning.	The teacher determines the goals of learning.
The teacher and learners develop individual and group learning plans.	The teacher may develop a learning plan.
Learners help monitor their progress and provide feedback to each other.	The teacher monitors the learners' progress.
Independence and collaboration are fostered.	Dependence and competition are fostered.
Instruction is learner-centered.	Instruction is teacher-centered.
The teacher and learners engage in dialogues.	The teacher and learners engage in monologues.

feedback to each other. In authoritarian education, either intentionally or as a side effect, dependence and competition are fostered. Learners in authoritarian systems may not trust their capacity to direct their own learning, and they tend to compete with each other for their teacher's favor.

Teachers who function collaboratively don't demand that learners function collaboratively from the start. Rather, they begin wherever their learners are, even if that means accommodating to learners who are dependent and passive. Collaborative teachers recognize that fostering their students' capacities as learners is a central responsibility, so, as soon as possible, these teachers encourage and help their learners assume more control of and responsibility for their learning. Authoritarian instructors, on the other hand, tend to be rigid about the pattern of their relationships with learners. They are likely to be threatened by and demeaning toward students who want some control over their learning. Collaborative teachers encourage learners to work with each other toward common goals. Authoritarian teachers often pit learners against each other.[1]

INFORMATION TEACHERS NEED

In the teacher-centered authoritarian model, teachers tend mostly to lecture, even when in small groups. They are not unlike traditional preachers. They spend a lot of time telling and showing while learners listen and watch. What they tell and show and how they provide information doesn't vary much from one group of learners to another; it is based chiefly on what they think learners should know, not on any information they have gathered about the learners' actual needs or their levels of readiness.

In the learner-centered collaborative model, on the other hand, teachers function largely as facilitators and coaches. Although collaborative teachers do some telling and showing, they spend even more time observing learners as they practice the intellectual, personal, and psychomotor capabilities they need as professionals (in simulated and real-world settings). And they ask

---

[1]*The conditions for lasting learning and the rationale for adopting a collaborative approach to teaching and patient care are documented, explained, and developed far more fully in our earlier book in this series (Westberg & Jason, 1993).*

thoughtful questions of learners and engage them in discussions and self-critiques. *What* they tell and show—including the feedback they provide to learners—and *how* they convey information varies from group to group, even from learner to learner. As much as possible they try to tailor what they do to the unique experiences, characteristics, and identified needs of each learner. (Most of us want nothing less for ourselves whenever we put ourselves in the position of being a learner; as when learning a new sport or a musical instrument.)

To be collaborative teachers who can provide learners with the experiences they need and feedback that guides their learning, we need information about our learners (e.g., what they already know, how they think through problems, how they interact with patients and other health professionals, how they handle health care challenges, how they feel when faced with various people and dilemmas). Put another way, because we are helping learners acquire a performing art, we have to see them perform at the outset of our work with them and at regular intervals thereafter.

Written examinations can provide us with information about some aspects of what learners know. But most written examinations don't give us much, if any, information about how they use what they know. And written examinations typically give us very little or no useful information about their *process* skills—how they think through problems, interact with others, or use their intellectual or personal skills.

To gather information on our learners' process skills, we need to hear them think out loud, we need to observe them in action as they face real-world challenges, and we need access to their invisible processes—what they are thinking and feeling as they engage in these real-world challenges. As we discuss shortly, video enables us to provide learners with practice opportunities in the classroom so that we can observe them in action. Reviewing video recordings of their work—in the classroom or in clinical settings—enables us to have enhanced access to their processes, both visible and invisible.

VIDEO RESOURCES

In this book we recommend a variety of video resources that can support and enhance teaching. The following is an overview of some of these resources.

Professionally Produced Programs

Many teachers are aware of the full-length video programs that have been created for use in health professions education, at least in their own disciplines, so we address the use of these tapes only briefly (in Chapter 2). Video programs for health professions educators are available from publishing houses, professional societies and associations, and university health sciences centers. Many programs are listed on the National Library of Medicine's computer database, AVline, and in the *National Library of Medicine Audiovisual Catalog*. Information is also available on the National Institute of Health's Combined Health Information Database. Still other sources are *The Video Source Book* (Weiner, 1993) and *R. R. Bowker's Complete Video Directory* (1992). Also, a consortium of more than 50 U.S. university media libraries produces a catalog, *Educational Film/Video Locator of the Consortium of University Film Centers and R.R. Bowker and Company* (1990). This catalog lists thousands of educational videos, films, and audiotapes that are available from the participating institutions for minimal borrowing costs. (The resources above are available at most libraries in schools of the health professions and/or general university libraries.)

Many full-length programs that were created for general audiences (not health professionals in particular) can be useful in health professions teaching. They include programs that were created specifically for the videocassette market, programs that were broadcast on television, and feature films that are available on videocassette. A librarian at your institution can probably help you locate useful programs and secure any permissions you may need for showing them in the classroom. For a list of feature films available on videotape that have been used in teaching psychosocial aspects of health care, see Alexander, Hall, and Pettice (1994).

Video Clips

Although there are times when it is useful to show full-length programs to learners, having them sit passively watching an extended program doesn't usually provide an optimal learning experience. You can help them to be more engaged and to derive more from the experience by providing them with one or more challenges before they watch a program (e.g., some questions to reflect on as they watch the program) and by conducting a discussion following the viewing of the program. However, the typical class or conference period seldom allows sufficient time for both showing a full-length program and having a good discussion.

In Chapter 2 we discuss using brief video clips (typically, up to about 10 minutes long) during small or large group sessions to illustrate and demonstrate topics that need to be brought to life or issues and events that learners need to visualize. Video clips can be segments extracted from full-length programs or brief images or events that may or may not be complete (e.g., a brief interview with a patient, some glimpses of an emergency room, a segment from a laboratory experiment). We devote Chapter 3 to a subset of video clips we call *video triggers*. In short, video triggers are brief (often less than 2 minutes long), usually incomplete events (vignettes) that are used for stimulating discussion, provoking intellectual and emotional reactions, and giving learners practice in dealing with tough challenges. Video clips can capture your students' and residents' attention and get them involved in their learning.

Recordings of You or Other Health Professionals Engaged in Health Care Activities

In Chapter 2 we discuss having recordings made of yourself as you demonstrate some of the capabilities your learners need to develop. Then we explore reviewing these recordings with your learners, focusing on both the visible and invisible processes in which you are engaged. The kinds of recordings we are recommending are not elaborate and can be made with inexpensive, consumer-level equipment (see below).

Recordings of Learners Engaged in Real or Simulated Health Care Activities

In Chapter 4 we discuss making recordings of learners as they role play the capabilities they are trying to develop (e.g., interviewing or counseling a patient; doing a clinical or laboratory procedure). In Chapter 5 we give step-by-step suggestions for videotaping learners as they engage in patient care or other clinical tasks in real health care settings. Again, these recordings do not have to be elaborate and can be done with consumer-level equipment.

VIDEO EQUIPMENT

Equipment Needed for Showing Video Clips or Longer Video Programs

Standard equipment for reviewing video recordings includes the following:

- one or more television monitors that are large enough to be seen easily by all members of the group (a loose rule of thumb: one 25-inch monitor for each 25 people)
- a stand for each monitor (for large groups, a good video projector is more desirable than several monitors: the larger the image, the greater the visual and emotional impact of the presentation)
- a video playback unit, preferably with a capacity for good-quality *freeze-frame*[2] and *visual scanning* (which enables you to see the picture fairly clearly as you fast-forward or rewind the tape when searching for specific segments)
- a remote control (preferably wireless) with pause and visual scan controls.

To determine the size of the screens you need for your monitor(s), note that the maximum acceptable viewing distance from a monitor is loosely tied to the diagonal measurement of the screen in inches. The rule of thumb: up to 1 foot from the monitor for each diagonal inch of screen measurement. For example, if the screen measures 25 inches diagonally, the acceptable viewing distance from that screen is up to 25 feet. If the video contains much text materials, then it is usually best for the learners to sit even closer. As we discuss in Chapter 2, the equipment you use for reviewing recordings needs to be compatible with the *format* of the video recordings (for VHS tapes, you need a VHS player; for 8mm tapes, an 8mm player, and so on).

---

[2]*Whenever we introduce technical video terms, we place them in italics. All such terms are defined in the Glossary at the end of the book.*

Equipment Needed for Reviewing Recordings in Supervisory Sessions

When reviewing recordings of learners' clinical activities (e.g., a counseling session or an interview of a patient) with one learner or a small group of learners, you need the same equipment as listed above, although a single monitor is sufficient.

Equipment Needed for Making Recordings

Video equipment is available in three arbitrary, imprecise categories: (1) consumer, (2) educational/industrial, and (3) professional. Your institution may have educational/industrial or professional-level equipment, but for making the recordings we discuss in this book, consumer-level equipment is satisfactory. In fact, some of the lightweight, compact, high-end consumer equipment (e.g., Hi8) is now so good that it is being used at times by professionals for videotaping in cramped, busy environments, such as emergency rooms.

The basic equipment you need:

- a *camcorder* (combination camera and recorder) with a zoom lens and replay capability, or separate camera and video recording units
- a *tripod*
- videotapes that are compatible with the camcorder/recorder you will be using
- possibly, supplementary lighting and microphones.

In Chapter 5 we discuss equipment needs and provide suggestions for making recordings.

CLASSROOM TEACHING AND CLINICAL SUPERVISION

For decades many students in the health professions spent almost all of the initial phase of their education in classrooms listening passively to lectures and in laboratories doing or witnessing laboratory exercises. Then they would move on to their clinical experiences. Today many schools provide learners with clinical experiences earlier in their education. During their clinical experiences students spend part of their time in classrooms and conference rooms, so now there is less of a sharp demarcation between the settings and processes used in preclinical and clinical studies (i.e., between classroom teaching and clinical supervision).

In this book, when we speak of *clinical supervision*, we mean the direct supervision of learners as they care for patients or engage in other clinical activities, typically during a clerkship, practicum, rotation, or other *clinical learning experience* (CLE). Some of these instructional activities are also referred to as *precepting*. The strategy we're recommending of sitting together with learners and jointly reviewing recordings of their clinical performance usually takes place in a precepting room or another room located in or close to the clinical setting, such as a small conference room.

When we speak of *classroom teaching*, we are referring to most of the teaching that takes place apart from the direct supervision of learners in clinical settings. This includes teaching that occurs in lecture halls and classrooms in health professions schools as well as the teaching that occurs in health care settings.

USING VIDEO TO HELP PROVIDE THE CONDITIONS FOR LASTING LEARNING

Finding ways to ensure that we are providing the conditions for lasting learning (discussed earlier in this chapter) is a dominant challenge for serious teachers. Here we summarize the ways that video can be a substantial help in meeting this challenge.

An Understanding of the Challenges and Tasks Learners Will Face in Their Future Work

Most of our learners are enrolled in our schools and programs because they are action-oriented people who see themselves as preparing to provide health care. When required to sit through numerous preclinical courses, many of them become restless to get involved with the real world of health care. In addition, learners who have not yet had many—or any—patient care experiences of their own may not understand how the topics we address in classrooms help them prepare for their future work.

Video enables you to bring health care events into the classroom, adding reality and relevance to the topics and issues you and your learners address. In Chapters 2–4 we discuss how you can use video triggers and other video clips to confront learners with real-world challenges, such as questions that patients and their family members ask and problems they present. And we discuss ways to use role playing for helping learners experience the challenges they need to be ready to deal with.

When learners are participating in clinical learning experiences, they are typically confronted with some of the challenges they will face in their future careers. When you and your learners review video recordings of their clinical work, you can help them reflect more deeply on those challenges (Chapter 6). As they review recordings of their peers' work, they can be exposed to challenges that their peers had that they haven't yet experienced themselves, and they can discuss these challenges with each other (Chapter 8).

Clarity about the Capabilities They Need

In some clinical settings, learners are exposed to people who are doing the things they need to learn. Sometimes, when providing this role-model function while engaged in patient care, we can stop and explain what we're doing. But that isn't always possible. Even when we're doing a formal demonstration in a classroom or a clinical setting, although learners can see and hear what we're doing, they can't, without our assistance, have access to our invisible processes—what we are thinking and feeling while engaged in those tasks. If we are demonstrating a skill that doesn't require much communication with a patient or others, it may be possible for us to articulate our invisible processes as they occur. If, however, we're demonstrating a skill that requires that we communicate with a patient or others, we can't simultaneously do that task and verbalize our invisible processes for our learners.

In Chapter 3 we discuss videotaping our demonstrations and then, as we review the recordings with our learners, stopping the tape at key points to discuss what we were thinking and feeling. We also talk about introducing learners to other role models by having them watch video recordings of those role models in action and then discussing the capabilities being demonstrated.

Opportunities for Systematic, Sequenced, Supervised Practice

In clinical settings, learners can usually practice many of their needed skills, but they can't always have the experiences they most need, and it's not always appropriate for them to practice with real patients. For example, the learners may be beginners who are not yet ready to work with patients, or the learners may be advanced students who want to experiment with a variety of approaches.

There can be advantages to teaching in classrooms and conference rooms. There we can create specific experiences for our learners and control some aspects of the learning environment. In Chapter 3 we discuss ways we can use video triggers to help learners practice dealing with instructional challenges. In Chapter 4 we explore how learners can practice new skills and refine existing ones through role playing with each other or with simulated patients.

Opportunities to Reflect on and Assess Their Work

For learners to reflect on and assess their work, they need to pause and examine what they have done. Video is one of the most powerful tools for enabling learners do this. Reviewing recordings of themselves engaged in role plays (Chapter 4) or in real clinical activities (Chapters 6–9) allows them to have the unique and potentially powerful opportunity of seeing themselves as others (particularly patients) see them. The recording prompts them to recall what they were thinking and feeling so that they and you (if they do their reflecting aloud) have access to their invisible processes. And they can review the event multiple times, enabling them to analyze their work in detail. Also, if they keep all or parts of the recordings of themselves, they can develop a *video log* of their work, enabling them to have the instructionally valuable experience of reviewing their progress over time (see Chapter 6).

Constructive Feedback on Their Efforts

When learners respond aloud to video triggers, we gain access to their thinking and, to some extent, to what they would say and do in various situations. This information enables us to give them feedback that is linked to their performance. As we work with learners in reviewing videotapes of their role-plays (Chapter 4) or their real clinical work (Chapters 6 and 7), we can link our feedback to what they have said and done. Abstract feedback ("You did a good job") isn't usually helpful. With video recordings, we can actually show them what we are talking about.

In clinical settings, because of our busy schedules and our learners' needs to work independently, we can't always observe our learners. Video recordings enable us to observe our learners when we are free to do so, and we can review the recordings multiple times if necessary. When we review recordings of our learners' work, our feedback can be based on our own observations rather than on our learners' reports of what they did, which, as we explain in Chapter 6, can be unintentionally flawed.

Throughout their education, learners need feedback from others. In Chapters 4 and 8 we discuss ways learners can get feedback from peers. In Chapter 9 we explore ways learners can get feedback from patients as they jointly review recordings of their interactions.

A Trust-based Relationship with Us and Their Peers

Trust is essential for using video effectively. For many learners the experience of watching and responding to video triggers and the experience of reviewing recordings of their work can, like a strong medication, have positive or negative consequences. Skilled educators can help individual learners or groups of learners use video triggers and recordings of their work to develop insights about their attitudes, feelings, and capabilities, including their strengths and areas needing further work. In unskilled or uncaring hands, these same recordings can be used to humiliate learners and can result in long-term negative consequences. If you earn your learners' trust when using video, they are likely to also trust you in other kinds of instructional encounters, enabling you to be more effective in those settings as well.

ISSUES AND CONSIDERATIONS

The power of video is linked to the knowledge and capabilities of the person using it.

Although it is potentially powerful, video ultimately is just a tool. As we discuss below, the effectiveness of video in support of any instruction you offer depends on your knowledge and skills, as a professional in your primary discipline, and as an educator.

Using video skillfully requires an understanding of the processes of the components of health care that you teach.

If you are to help learners understand the processes that your discipline engages in when contributing to some aspect of health care, you need to be critically aware of these processes yourself. To this end, you might want to tape yourself engaged in the activities you want your learners to be able to do. (If you are a basic scientist, we hope you agree that your most important accomplishments and the contributions you most need to make to your students are not the facts to which you may have access but the intellectual skills you bring to bear on issues and problems—in a word, the *processes*, not the *conclusions*, of science.) Then review these tapes, by yourself or with colleagues, reflecting not only on what you were doing but also on what you were thinking and feeling. In addition, you might want to read literature in your field that focuses on the process of care or problem solving. For example, in nursing, considerable attention has been paid to the nursing process (e.g., Alfaro, 1986; Yura & Walsh, 1983). In medicine there is a growing interest in the process of problem-solving (e.g., Elstein, Shulman, & Sprafka, 1978; the regular feature, "Clinical Problem-Solving," in the *New England Journal of Medicine*).

Using video skillfully requires an understanding of the processes of learning.

People learn in a variety of ways. In general, though, we can facilitate learning for most people by providing them with the conditions for lasting learning described above and by relating to them in collaborative ways. We deal more fully with these issues later.

Using video effectively requires a variety of instructional capabilities.

Using video triggers requires group facilitation skills. So does helping a group of learners review recordings of each other's work. Supervising individual learners in critiquing video recordings of their work requires an understanding of the steps involved in effective one-on-one supervision. Later in this book we discuss the specific instructional capabilities needed for using video in these ways and in the other ways that we propose.

Video is most effective when used in dynamic, interactive ways.

Typically, teachers play video programs in their entirety to a largely passive group of learners. Following the playing of a program, which often is 20 minutes or longer, the teacher might engage students in a discussion of the program they watched. Although this approach may sometimes be appropriate, most people learn best when they can reflect on and react to smaller chunks of new information. As when listening to lectures, learners who are passively watching a video program tend to "tune out" after relatively short periods. Throughout this book we propose numerous ways to use video in smaller chunks and in more dynamic ways.

Video equipment is becoming increasingly user-friendly.

Not too many years ago, making and using video in the ways we are proposing was a major production, involving large, bulky equipment and considerable technical expertise. It was not the domain of amateurs, and experts were typically needed. Although you may still prefer to turn to the audiovisual experts at your institution for help in making and using recordings, video equipment is now so much more compact and easy to use that virtually anyone can make acceptable recordings for many instructional uses. Some camcorders (combination cameras and recorders) weigh less than two pounds. The newer equipment requires little or no auxiliary lighting or extra microphones for most of the in-house uses we are recommending. Knowing how to use the equipment and managing it yourself allows you to exert more control over the processes of making and reviewing recordings while avoiding strains on limited budgets.

SUMMARY

Learning, as is no news to seasoned teachers, doesn't just happen. Merely getting up and talking at learners is of little value for complex learning and by itself has little if any lasting value. Much like providing high-quality health care, providing high-quality instruction requires professionals who make a special effort to ensure that those being served are provided with whatever it is that they most need. Learners need a set of explicit conditions. Serious teachers, who hope to have a sustained impact on learners, are in constant search of strategies, tactics, and resources for enhancing their effectiveness in meeting the conditions that their learners need. As we have noted in this chapter, video technology, when used with skill and care, may be the most potent support technology currently available for helping to provide the conditions that learners need. Of equal importance, the diminishing cost, the increasing ease of use, and the steadily growing capabilities of this technology now place it within easy reach of most educators in the health professions while enabling decent quality, educationally useful, products in the hands of users with limited experience. The issues introduced in this chapter are expanded upon in the rest of this book.

PART I

Using Video in the Classroom

Teaching in classrooms presents many challenges: getting and sustaining our learners' attention, helping them understand the relevance of the topics and issues we address, getting them to be active participants in class and in their learning, and more. But teaching in classrooms also has a major advantage. We can shape the environment (within limits), producing educational experiences that prepare leaners for and complement the experiences they have in health care settings.

The classroom is like our own small theater. Unless we're in a room with installed seating, we can arrange the furniture in ways that best suit our purposes. We can bring in props and scripts. We can invite learners to rehearse tasks they will face, and we can ask them to try taking on the roles of patient, family member, colleague, and others.

In this environment, video enhances our capacity to provide learners with the conditions needed for lasting learning. We can bring images and challenges from the real world into the classroom (Chapters 2 and 3). We can illustrate, model, and demonstrate the capabilities they need to develop (Chapter 2). By using video triggers (Chapter 3) or by engaging learners in role playing with simulated patients/clients (Chapters 3 and 4), we can give them opportunities to practice needed capabilities and reflect on and critique their performance. And we can give them feedback on their efforts.

CHAPTER 2

Using Video for Illustrating, Modeling, and Demonstrating

In the early stages of learning, most students don't have clear images of the tasks and challenges they will face in their future work or of the capabilities they will need for responding effectively to those tasks and challenges. Although some have generalized notions based on their life experiences or the popular media, most beginners have not had meaningful exposure to the full array of people they will care for, the health care needs of these people, the settings in which they will work, the kinds of decisions they will need to make, what they will have to be prepared to say and do, the knowledge and skills they need for being effective in their work, the capabilities of the other professionals with whom they will work, or the resources they will have at their disposal. Yet to be active participants in their own learning—to be meaningfully engaged in formulating their learning goals and developing plans for achieving those goals—they need detailed images of the world they are entering and of the kind of professional they want to become.

To provide our learners with these images, we need to *illustrate* key elements of the world they are entering; *model* the behaviors they need to adopt (or show them images of others modeling these behaviors); and *demonstrate* the execution of the tasks and processes involved in functioning successfully (both the visible and the invisible capabilities they need to develop). Video enables us to illustrate for our learners the world they are entering and to provide models and demonstrations of the behaviors and capabilities they will need.

In this chapter, we

- explore using video for illustrating, modeling, and demonstrating
- examine some reasons for making recordings of your demonstrations and reviewing them with learners
- explore some issues and considerations to have in mind when using video for illustrating, modeling, and demonstrating
- provide explicit suggestions for (1) preparing for demonstrations; (2) reviewing your video recordings with learners; and (3) videotaping interviews you do of patients or others.

ILLUSTRATING, MODELING, AND DEMONSTRATING

Although illustrating, modeling, and demonstrating are related and overlapping strategies, distinct instructional tasks can be highlighted by thinking about them individually.

Illustrating the World of Health Care

The ancient aphorism is probably right: a picture can be worth a thousand words. For decades educators of health professionals have used slides, slide-tape combinations, overhead transparencies, chalkboard drawings, film, and other audio-visual aids to illustrate the content of their lectures and other presentations. All of these audio-visuals are still useful, but as growing numbers of teachers are finding, video can illustrate and represent some events and issues more effectively than static slides, overheads, or chalkboard drawings, and it is far easier to use than film.

Video lends itself particularly well to events in which learners need to

- observe movement (e.g., the gait of a child with cerebral palsy; the sequence of events in a complex laboratory experiment)
- study movements in slow motion (e.g., rapid physiological changes in a laboratory experiment)

- hear the sounds that accompany images (e.g., coughs, heart sounds)
- hear and see people with various affects (e.g., anxious, depressed)
- listen to people talking
- witness and study nonverbal behavior
- get a sense of the sights, sounds, and atmospheres of various environments (e.g., emergency rooms, operating rooms, intensive care units).

With the growing availability of video recordings made during laparoscopic and endoscopic surgeries, learners can also have access to views of the interior of the living human body that were not available to prior generations.

Most of our learners grew up watching television, so they are accustomed to, and even expect to see, video images. Unlike earlier generations who grew up listening to the radio, our learners anticipate being shown, rather than only being told. And, of course, some information is conveyed far more effectively by being shown than by only being explained. Learners can much more rapidly grasp the look, sound, and emotional impact of a person who is depressed by seeing and listening to a depressed person than by only hearing a description of the condition. Seeing images, rather than just listening to someone talk about situations or events, gives learners a chance to make their own observations and generate their own hypotheses—two central tasks of active learning.

Video enables us to illustrate some procedures, processes, and findings that students have traditionally learned in the laboratory. With decreasing resources and the shrinking time available for teaching the basic sciences, it is not possible for students to have all the laboratory experiences that might be helpful to them. Video enables teachers to bring some of those experiences to the classroom. And video enables teachers to edit together clips of events that occur over extended periods of time, reducing events from hours or days to minutes.

Learners are likely to get the most out of watching a video clip or a full-length video program if you prepare them for watching it. For example, giving them questions or issues to ponder, or a specific challenge or assignment, can help focus their attention:

> As you watch this brief program on health care in the United States, think through how the issues that are raised apply to our community.

Or:

> Today we're going to be studying the anatomy of the hand. To appreciate the beauty and complexity of the hand, I want to show you some brief images of people using their hands for various everyday activities. As you watch hands being used for bathing, eating, dressing, writing, and other activities, think through what internal design features of the hand may be needed for enabling these capabilities.

If you show a video clip that is taken from a larger program, you need to establish the context and give credit to the producers. In the next chapter we deal with these and other issues when we provide specific suggestions for preparing to use video triggers.

Modeling Behaviors

To prepare for becoming professionals, learners need a general sense of what they will be doing, ranging from motor skills they will perform to how they will carry themselves. This understanding comes best from observing others who are already doing what they are about to learn. Many beginning students, however, spend much of the early part of their education being taught by people who are not clinicians, and they have few opportunities to observe health professionals in action. Once they are in clinical environments, learners can observe health professionals at work, but they still don't always have opportunities to observe fully relevant role models. And in the busy world of health care, learners seldom get to linger for sufficient time next to clinicians doing complex tasks or procedures.

With video we can provide learners with vivid images of a variety of professionals engaged in both routine and unusual tasks. Exposing learners to practicing professionals is certainly not done with the intent of producing exact replicas of some idealized model. Rather, the purpose is to offer a range of options from which learners can begin choosing, as they form their own professional identities and approaches.

Since most of us identify most easily with people who are similar to us, learners who are forming their identities and refining their early skills are also helped by observing role models who are not too far removed from where they are; models who are still in training and faced with similar but more advanced challenges. In addition, students and residents can sometimes understand behavior more fully if, in addition to seeing examples of people modeling desirable, effective ways of behaving, they can also witness less effective examples (Parrish & Babbitt, 1991). Although few faculty members are likely to volunteer as the designated negative role models, exposure to a wide range of people tends to assure that some suboptimal examples will be available to serve as needed counterpoints.

Modeling and video-modeling have been shown to be of value to learners in both the beginning and advanced stages of skill acquisition (e.g., Dowrick & Jesdale, 1991; Hall & Errfmeyer, 1983; Ross, Bird, Doody, & Zoeller, 1985) and in the learning of sports (Franks & Maile, 1991). Just as persons learning to ski or play tennis can get a sense of what they need by watching videotapes of professional athletes in action, so can health professionals begin acquiring a picture of what they need by watching videos of health professionals engaging in relevant tasks, particularly if the camerawork draws the viewer's attention to key elements of those tasks.

What learners are able to perceive and absorb, however, depends in large part on their level of experience with the characteristics or skills being modeled. Beginners observing a videotape of a skilled counseling session, for example, will perceive far less than will a skilled counselor. And learners are likely to get much more out of video-modeling if you prepare them for what they will be seeing (e.g., give them particular details to look for) and if you review what they have seen after they view the video.

Demonstrating Capabilities Learners Need to Develop

Learners who are in the early stages of acquiring complex skills can seldom perceive, absorb, and remember more than part of what the models to whom they are exposed have done. They are unlikely to notice the nuances of complex procedures and seldom retain sufficient detail to guide their own practice of these new skills. Under the best of modeling situations, they still don't have access to the experts' invisible processes: what they were thinking or feeling as they did the procedure, performed the experiment, solved the problem, talked with the patient, counseled the family members, or engaged in other complicated activities.

To move forward in developing a complex skill, learners usually need us to demonstrate the details of the skill. (Later, of course, they need to practice the skill, engage in self-assessment, and receive feedback.) Often this means we need to slow down the process, simplify it, break it into its component parts, highlight important details, repeat complex maneuvers and actions, and clearly explain what we are doing. And we may need to articulate our invisible processes.

As we discuss more fully below, videotaped recordings of your demonstrations can help you accomplish these instructional tasks. Video recordings of demonstrations can be made and used in a variety of ways. You can be recorded while performing some skills in their natural setting, with or without learners present. Then, in a classroom or conference room, you can review the tape with learners. Reviewing the tape alone, before reviewing it with your learners, enables you to identify the segments you want to highlight.

You can also enhance your demonstrations with video by being taped while doing a demonstration for learners. If it will be difficult for learners to see or hear any part of the demonstration, it can be fed to video monitors while it is being recorded. If appropriate, you can ask the videographer to get close-up views of some of what you are doing. Following the demonstration, you can review the tape of the demonstration with the learners, dwelling as needed on difficult or confusing elements.

You can also turn to professionally produced video-based demonstrations, which are available on a variety of topics. Many teachers have used such tapes, so we won't discuss their use here, except to emphasize the value of playing some of these tapes in stages, with breaks for comments and questions, rather than playing them straight through without interruption. Multiple pauses are especially important for tapes that depict complex skills or for those demonstrations that are too fast-paced for your audience's level of readiness.

Another strategy is available to you, if you have a large group of students who have television monitors near their work stations (e.g., laboratory tables, simulators) and are able to immediately practice the skill(s) you are teaching. You can be videotaped while demonstrating steps that the students need to take and then inviting the students to ask questions and practice those steps themselves. If it's feasible and the students need extra help, you can review certain steps before proceeding. The recording of your demonstration can be kept for review by students who need even further help.

REASONS FOR REVIEWING RECORDINGS OF YOUR DEMONSTRATIONS WITH LEARNERS

You can break complex skills into manageable chunks.

Learners who are trying to acquire a complex skill tend to be overwhelmed if given too much information too quickly. With video recordings, you can break skills into their component parts, showing one step at a time. After showing each step you can pause the tape, ask questions of your learners, and even, if feasible, give them opportunities to practice the step you just demonstrated while you observe and supervise them.

You can repeat segments.

When learners observe a demonstration of a complex skill, they cannot always grasp what they need in a single viewing. With video recordings, you can repeat difficult elements or steps in a skill as often as needed.

You can slow down or freeze the action.

The components of some skills occur too quickly to be fully perceived and grasped, especially by beginners. Using the still-frame and slow-motion capabilities available on most contemporary better-quality video playback units, you can slow down and freeze actions, even those that can't readily be slowed down in real life. With any equipment, you can stop the tape frequently, allowing learners to digest what they've just seen before moving on.

Reviewing your recordings with learners enables you to discuss your internal processes—to make the invisible visible.

Although it is possible to explain your internal processes while you are engaged in some tasks, particularly those tasks requiring little or no communication with others while being done, most demonstrations are likely to be too preoccupying for you to be both doing the task at hand and explaining your thoughts and feelings. Many demonstrations can be made much more successful by being video-recorded. You can then review the recording with your learners, stopping the tape at key points to discuss the thoughts and feelings you had during the segment they just saw.

You can model strategies for reflecting on and verbalizing your internal processes.

In Chapter 6 we discuss strategies for helping learners use video recordings of their work with patients to help them reflect on and verbalize their internal processes. If they have observed you reflecting on your work and articulating your thoughts and feelings, they will be more likely to, and be better equipped for, exercising these important skills for themselves. In other words, when using video and reflection as part of your demonstrations, you are accomplishing two sets of instructional goals: you are enhancing the effectiveness of your teaching of the task at hand, and you are helping to prepare your learners for an important element of their future learning.

You can replay a recording multiple times, focusing on a different issue each time.

The early stages of most learning—especially the learning of complex, multilevel skills, such as those involved in relating to patients or others—tend to proceed best when learners can focus on one issue or theme at a time. Video enables us to review events multiple times so that separate themes or issues can be isolated for special attention at each viewing. For example, during your first review of a tape demonstrating a clinical encounter you might talk with your learners about the kinds of questions you asked the patient. During the second viewing you might focus on the patient's verbal and nonverbal communication.

Learners can review the tape again after the demonstration session.

Many learners are helped in acquiring new skills by sequentially observing a demonstration of the skill, practicing the skill, and then observing the demonstration again as a cross-check on the practice they did. When learners first try doing an examination or procedure, they can encounter problems or develop questions that can be answered by re-viewing the recorded demonstration. Your taped demonstrations can be made available to learners in a library, learning resource center, or other site (e.g., Lincoln, Layton, & Holdman, 1978).

ISSUES AND CONSIDERATIONS

You can extract video clips from existing footage.

In our discussion of video triggers in the next chapter, we suggest some sources from which to extract video clips (e.g., television documentaries, films that are available on videocassettes). We also explore some of the steps you need to take (e.g., assure that your intended use is acceptable, or secure the permission of the producer) when using certain materials. It is usually relatively easy to comply with the copyright laws when using materials for educational purposes.

You can make your own video clips.

If you enjoy making videos, you can create your own clips. Some of the suggestions we offer in Chapter 5 might help. If you need more extensive help with making your own videos, there are several sources you can consult (see the section "Further Readings in Video Production" at the end of Chapter 5). Depending on the images and sounds you want to make available to your learners, you can make video recordings in the community, in health centers, in hospitals, in laboratories, and elsewhere. You can record other people in action, and you can shoot your own interviews of patients and others. Below, in "Videotaping Your Interviews Yourself," we make some suggestions for how to record your own interviews.

The elaborateness of tapes you make of your demonstrations can vary enormously.

The video recordings that teachers make of their demonstrations range from simple, unedited recordings made with inexpensive video equipment to complex edited programs created with professional-level equipment. Some elaborately edited programs include sophisticated graphics. Factors to consider when deciding on how elaborate to make your recorded demonstrations include:

- whether your instructional goals require a sophisticated production
- whether you will use the recording or program once or multiple times
- whether you will make the recording available for learners to view on their own
- whether you want to make the recording available to other teachers for their use
- whether you want to use the recording at a major conference or other event where high production values are expected
- your financial resources.

If you want a straightforward recording to use on one or two occasions for an informal demonstration to a group of learners, you can probably get by with a simple, unedited recording made with inexpensive, consumer-level equipment. If, however, you need to use graphics and want to use an edited program for multiple audiences, you probably need a more elaborate production. Some schools help support productions made for educational purposes. Many don't. Since video productions can be expensive, your financial resources or other forms of support can be a crucial factor in your planning.

Simply videotaping a demonstration won't assure that it will be effective.

For a video recording of a demonstration to be maximally helpful, it needs to be based on an effective demonstration in the first place. Some of the following characteristics of effective demonstrations were introduced earlier. Most of the characteristics listed below are elaborated on later in the chapter.

Effective demonstrations of complex skills

- include an overview of the skill (learners need to see the skill modeled)
- break the skill into its component parts
- are paced for the learners' levels of readiness
- include repetition, as necessary
- highlight or magnify important details and potential challenges
- include all necessary information but avoid an overload of material
- present information as clearly as possible
- include opportunities for learners to ask questions
- include opportunities for learners to practice the skill, if possible.

Learners need a sense of the big picture, of the entire capability they will seek to master. This is particularly true for elaborate, multipart skills, such as interviewing or counseling, that must be seen in their entirety for the individual steps to have meaning. (This can be accomplished prior to the demonstration by having the learners see the skill modeled by others, either live or on video.)

When teaching complex, multipart skills (e.g., the complete physical examination or physical assessment), after assuring that learners have a sense of the big picture, it is usually best to work with them on one component at a time (e.g., vital signs, the cardiovascular exam). Even some of these segments need to be broken into their component parts. For example, after demonstrating the full cardiovascular exam, you can demonstrate each of its parts, pausing between parts for learners to ask questions and to practice what you have demonstrated. Beginners can be helped to grasp fast-paced skills by seeing all or part of the skill at a slower than normal pace.

Beginners can easily become overwhelmed by too much information. Particularly when first demonstrating a new skill to beginners, it's important to be sensitive to signs that learners are experiencing an overload. Unfamiliar technical language can confuse learners. New terms need to be defined. Explanations need to be succinct and to the point.

Some health professionals fail to do effective demonstrations because they are "unconsciously competent."

We are indebted to Whitman & Schwenk (1984) for citing an article (*Personnel Journal*, 1974) that describes stages people tend to go through when developing new skills. We have observed these four stages in ourselves, our colleagues, and our learners:

1. unconsciously incompetent
2. consciously incompetent
3. consciously competent
4. unconsciously competent

Typically, when we first approach a new skill we are *unconsciously incompetent*. We are so new at the task that we are unaware of what we need and do not realize the specific ways in which we are not competent. For example, when first learning to windsurf we might continually fall off the sailboard but be unaware of what we need to change to maintain our balance. Similarly, most new learners in the health professions cannot provide much of an answer to the question, "What do you most need to learn at this time?"

After some instruction in a new skill, we are still not particularly effective but now are aware of some of our limitations and what we need to work on. At this stage we have become *consciously incompetent*. In our windsurfing example, after some lessons we may still fall a lot but are now more aware of why we fall and what changes we need to make.

After more demonstrations, supervised practice, and feedback, we move to the third stage: we are *consciously competent*. We understand what is needed and can provide it. We not only know what it takes to stay on the windsurfer, but we are able to do what it takes to stay afloat, and the learning experience is still so fresh we can articulate the elements of the process.

After years of using new skills, most of us move to the fourth stage: we become *unconsciously competent*. We have lost track of the steps we took in developing the skill; we are performing it rather automatically and can no longer readily articulate the elements of the process for others. We are at risk of being insensitive to the plight and needs of beginners we may be trying to help.

Health professionals are usually asked to demonstrate certain skills because of their competence in using these skills. Many, however, have become unconsciously competent. They are likely to gloss over vital details and be less than optimally helpful to beginners.

Some health professionals use strategies and techniques in their demonstrations that are not optimal for beginners.

The techniques used by experts are not always appropriate for beginners. Professional athletes, for example, often "break the rules," performing their sport with their own variations on the fundamentals. They use shortcuts they adopted after first mastering the basics. Many devise styles that are best suited to their unique, advanced talents and body types. Some professionals also go through rituals that have more to do with their personal belief systems than with the technical performance of their sport.

Expert health professionals also break the rules and use shortcuts and systems that are best suited to their unique talents. For example, many expert clinicians are sufficiently perceptive in their observations of patients that they can telescope their interviews and exams of new patients without much risk of missing important information. Students with limited backgrounds and experience are not helped by demonstrations of these shortcuts. They can also be confused by the idiosyncratic styles of some expert clinicians. Most often, beginners first need to learn to do complex tasks in complete and conventional ways. And they need a foundation of experiences with these tasks before they start adopting modifications and shortcuts, however appropriate these timesavers may later be.

Simulated patients/clients can be useful resources.

Simulated patients/clients are actors or others who have been trained to present their health and personal histories (and sometimes physical findings) in particular ways. They may, for example, present with specific symptoms and affects. Simulated patients are particularly useful when demonstrating communications skills and some examinations and procedures. The advantages of using simulated patients for demonstrations include the following:

- not having to intrude upon real patients
- being able to "program" the patients so that they have the specific problems and personal characteristics needed for maximally effective demonstrations
- being able to adjust the level of difficulty of the learners' tasks to match their levels of readiness.

For example, if you want to demonstrate strategies for counseling anxious people, you can program a person to present as the type of anxious person who can help you demonstrate certain points. The disadvantages of using simulated patients for demonstrations include the time and effort involved in recruiting and training them, although once trained, they can be used repeatedly with multiple individuals and groups. (See Chapter 9 for a fuller discussion of simulated patients.)

SUGGESTIONS

PREPARING FOR DEMONSTRATIONS

The following suggestions are summarized in Appendix 2.1. Most of these suggestions also apply to doing demonstrations that are not videotaped.

- **Assess your learners' current capacities for doing the skill you intend to demonstrate.**

If you will be demonstrating a skill for learners whose backgrounds in that skill are not known to you, take time to find out about their prior experiences and their current levels of capability. Some questions you might ask them:

- Have you ever watched this skill being performed?
- What experience, if any, have you had doing this skill yourself?
- How competent do you feel you are at doing this skill?
- What kind of help do you think you need in learning this skill?

If the learners have already had some experience with the skill you are intending to demonstrate, consider asking them to demonstrate the skill to you. As they do, be aware of individual differences in specific areas, such as manual dexterity and confidence. Once you know their current capabilities, you can adapt your demonstration, as needed, to be optimally helpful in taking them from where they are to the next level of accomplishment.

- **Identify the steps you take when performing the skill you will demonstrate as well as the steps beginners need to take.**

If you suspect that you have become unconsciously competent in the skill you will teach, try recapturing the steps you went through when you first learned the skill. As best you can, reflect on the stumbling blocks you faced when you began. Even consider sharing some of your initial difficulties with your learners. Novices can be comforted by knowing that those who are now experts had some of the same problems that they do, when first learning this skill.

Because it is common for experts to have developed shortcuts and variations on basic techniques, you may find that your current way of doing whatever skills you will demonstrate is not appropriate for beginners. For example, imagine you will be teaching the physical examination or physical assessment. In your daily practice, you probably tailor what you do to each patient's unique needs, excluding steps in the exam you deem unnecessary during a particular encounter. However, you may decide that beginners first need to learn to do complete examinations before learning how to adapt the exam for each patient.

Carefully think through the steps that beginners need to take when acquiring the capabilities you want them to learn. Consider discussing these issues with some beginners or near-beginners as an aid in jogging your memory and to help you select the issues that deserve most attention.

- **Consider talking with learners who have recently mastered the skill you plan to demonstrate.**

People who have recently mastered a skill and are now consciously competent typically have fresh memories of which instructional and learning strategies were most and least helpful to them. If possible, ask learners who have recently acquired the skill you will be demonstrating what kind of demonstration they think will be most useful for beginners. Even consider asking one or more of these advanced learners to join you in demonstrating the skill to your beginning learners. During the demonstration, these advanced learners can share their insights with the beginners and even serve as liaisons between you and the students, if appropriate.

- **Reflect on the kind of demonstration that will be most helpful to your learners.**

Using your knowledge of the complexity of the skill you will demonstrate and your learners' levels of readiness for learning it, think through such issues as

- whether you should break the skill into its component parts
- how you should pace the presentation
- whether you should include some repetition
- whether there are some details you need to highlight or literally magnify with close-up video images
- how much information you should include
- how you can make your explanations as clear as possible.

Think through how you want to review the tape. Should you, for example, stop it every few minutes to articulate what you were thinking or feeling?

- **Identify and arrange for the people and resources you need for the demonstration.**

Decide whom you need to involve in the demonstration—a real or simulated patient, an assistant, other members of the health team?

And decide what equipment and other resources you will need. If you want learners to practice the skill immediately after you demonstrate it, you may need to think about equipment for learners as well as equipment for yourself. To avoid disappointment and problems, schedule people and resources well in advance of your demonstration.

- **If you will involve real or simulated patients, prepare them for the demonstration and secure their informed consent.**

Tell patients what you hope to accomplish and what you would like them to do. Let them know who will watch the demonstration and how the video recording will be used. Talk with patients about ways that you will ensure their comfort. Many patients appreciate knowing that they will be free to request a pause or can terminate the session if they become tired or uncomfortable. Approached with consideration and respect, we and others have found most patients eager to help.

When you videotape patients, most schools and institutions require that they sign a consent form. Many of these forms are written in obtuse legal language, so you might need to explain their meaning to patients. (If your institution uses confusing forms, consider requesting that they be rewritten in straightforward, easy-to-understand language.)

- **Arrange for your demonstration to be videotaped, and ensure that the camera operator knows what your learners need to see and hear.**

Smooth camera work requires that the camera operator is able to anticipate each shot so that she can make needed moves and adjustments. To ensure that the camera operator gets the shots you need, review with her what you intend to do. If you plan to sit relatively still, talking with a patient, videotaping will be easy. If, however, you will be moving around or need special shots, such as close-ups of certain maneuvers, then making a recording is more challenging. You can help the videographer to anticipate what she will need to do by having a "dry run" of the demonstration in advance. Show her where you will sit or stand and what moves you will make. If a patient will be involved, have the patient or a patient substitute go through the motions with you.

Many schools in the health professions have audio-visual technicians available for videotaping demonstrations and other presentations. If there are no experienced videographers available to you, consider having a colleague or student help with the recording.

- **Arrange for needed video equipment.**

If you are going to rent or reserve equipment, do so as far in advance as possible so that you can be sure that the equipment will be available when you need it.

- **If your demonstration will be taped in a clinical setting, make sure that the location is suitable and that personnel at the site have been alerted.**

Some patient care facilities have video recording equipment installed in exam rooms and in counseling or consulting rooms (see Chapter 5). If suitable video equipment is already installed in the setting in which you want to do your demonstration, you are fortunate. If not, make sure that the location you will use has electrical outlets for the video equipment and adequate space for the equipment and a camera operator. (If you are using a small portable camcorder, you will require minimal extra room.) In addition, be sure that health professionals and others whose work will be affected by your videotaping are made aware, in advance, of what you'll be doing.

REVIEWING RECORDED DEMONSTRATIONS WITH LEARNERS

The following suggestions are summarized in Appendix 2.2. As with all of our suggestions in this book, the following are recommendations for your consideration, not hard-and-fast rules. There are no precise recipes that can cover the wide variety of possible instructional goals and situations.

- **If you first did a live demonstration in front of the learners, invite their questions and comments before reviewing the tape.**

Teaching is usually most effective if it is linked to learners' needs and interests. Your learners' questions and comments can give you important clues about what they understand and what they need help with. This information can help guide your review of the tape.

- **If you won't be doing a live demonstration, consider first playing the videotaped demonstration in its entirety.**

As we've discussed, learners need a sense of the overall skill: the "big picture." If the videotaped demonstration isn't too long, consider playing the entire recording once before reviewing the tape in a more interactive way. After the initial viewing, you might, for example, stop every few minutes or after every discrete segment to discuss what you were doing and to raise questions.

- **Prepare the learners for the review of the tape.**

Tell your learners how you plan to review the tape. Many learners will not be accustomed to having teachers articulate their internal processes, so if you intend to do so, alert them to your planned approach. Consider asking them to speculate as to why it is important for you to discuss your internal processes.

- **Consider inviting learners to ask you to pause the tape when they have questions or concerns.**

Learners' questions and comments during demonstrations can help guide what you do. If it will not interrupt your planned approach, invite learners to signal when they have questions or concerns so that you can pause the tape and talk with them. If you ask learners to wait with their questions until you finish reviewing the entire tape, they might forget or dismiss their comments, and you might miss valuable instructional opportunities.

- **Pause the tape to discuss what you were thinking during key stages of the activity you are demonstrating.**

During many interactions with patients, our heads are busy with thoughts about such matters as our impressions of the patient, what we want to know, what we plan to do, and what we anticipate they will say and do. Particularly if we're deeply involved in a process, such as trying to identify or solve a problem, our learners can be helped by having access to the internal processes that accompanied the activity in which we were engaged.

- **Consider pausing at decision points to discuss optional strategies.**

While solving scientific or clinical problems, doing interviews, conducting counseling sessions, and performing certain exams and procedures, there are key decision points at which experienced professionals recognize that they have two or more options to select among. For example, at the opening of an interview with a patient who presents two reasons for coming to the clinic, your options include exploring whether she has additional agendas or concerns, asking her to elaborate on the first reason she presented, and asking her to elaborate on the second reason she presented.

Another example of a decision point can be seen in the following exchange:

Clinician: How can we help you today?
Patient: I've been having terrible headaches.

At this decision point the clinician (or the patient) could direct the interview in a variety of directions. The clinician, for example, could choose to be open-ended and inclusive:

Clinician: I'd like to hear about your headaches. But first, is there anything else you're hoping we'll deal with today?

The clinician could choose to be open-ended but focused:

Clinician: Tell me about your headaches.

The clinician could be more focused and ask a closed question:

Clinician: When do your headaches begin?

Or the clinician could keep the interview even more open by simply nodding and indicating an interest in hearing more, or by saying, "Please go on."

In many situations, although some options tend to be more productive than others, there may not be only one clearly right choice. Being a competent health professional involves becoming aware whenever you are at a key decision point, recognizing the full range of options available at that moment, and having a basis for selecting among those options. You can help learners begin identifying these decision points and build their armamentarium of options by inviting them to take the initiative in identifying the decision points in your demonstration and in suggesting and discussing the available options.

- **Pause the tape to discuss what you were feeling at key points during the demonstration, if appropriate.**

Typically, insufficient attention is given in health professions education to the impact of health professionals' attitudes and feelings about the care they render. Our feelings can be important clues about what is going on with a patient. For example, if you were feeling good before entering a patient's room but then began feeling depressed as you talked with the patient, your feelings might be a valuable clue about the patient's condition. Also, positive or negative feelings about patients can influence our decisions and conclusions, such as the amount of time we spend with them and how we interpret what they say or do. You can help learners begin to see the importance of their feelings by identifying and discussing yours and by talking about how you use your feelings in your interactions with patients.

- **Consider replaying segments of the demonstration multiple times.**

As we mentioned above, you can replay segments that were confusing to the learners. Also, each time you replay a segment you can focus on a different task. For example, the first time through you might focus on what you were doing. The second time you might focus on the patient.

- **Consider reviewing complex rapid maneuvers in slow motion.**

Using the *freeze-frame* and slow-motion capabilities of video playback units, you can help learners perceive the details of a wide variety of fast-moving events, such as emergency or "code" management, some laboratory procedures and experiments, and the subtleties of nonverbal behavior.

- **When you finish reviewing the recording, invite the learners' questions and comments.**

When observing the demonstration of a new skill, learners may need time to formulate questions. Even if you invited the learners' questions during your demonstration, invite their questions again after reviewing the recording of your demonstration.

- **As soon as possible provide opportunities for learners to practice.**

Learners' acquisition of new skills can be aided by early opportunities to practice the skills they saw demonstrated, while the demonstration is still fresh in their minds. If you are able to integrate their practice into the demonstration session, you can use their practice as a diagnostic opportunity. Your observations of what they have grasped and what they may need more help with can guide your decisions about what parts of the demonstration need to be repeated or emphasized and what misperceptions need to be corrected.

VIDEOTAPING YOUR INTERVIEWS YOURSELF

Here *interview* means either an interview you do with a patient or client, for diagnostic or therapeutic purposes as part of a health care interaction, or an interview that you do outside your role as a caregiver. For example, you might interview a school principal about the health of the children in her school, or you might talk with an elderly man about the health care he has received. The interviews could be used for illustrating, modeling, or demonstrating. The video image could include only the person you interview or both of you.

There are three ways you could tape such interviews. The first technique, which is rather awkward and should be used only under special circumstances, provides the viewers of your tape with the impression that the interviewee is talking directly to them. Using a lightweight camera on a tripod placed between you and your subject, or holding the *viewfinder* of the camera up to your eye and viewing your subject as you interact with him or her, you take a full-face, straight-on shot of your subject.

The second and third strategies involve putting the camera on a tripod and adjusting the framing so that you record either an image of only your subject or an image of both you and your subject. (Include yourself in the image if you want your learners to see you in action. If, for example, you are demonstrating the use of nonverbal communication in effective interviewing, your learners would need to see you.) Either strategy would result in an unchanging *point of view* throughout the interview because the camera would remain in a single, fixed position.

First steps with any of the strategies are explaining to your intended subject what you would like to do and getting his or her informed consent, preferably in writing.

The following are some steps to take when using the second or third strategy. Further suggestions for making recordings are in Chapter 5.

- **Ask the subject to sit in a chair that is placed near your chair.**

The chairs should not swivel or move easily. It can be very annoying to watch a video of someone steadily rocking or swiveling in a chair, which some people are prone to do if the chair permits. The chairs should be placed so that you and the subject can carry on a conversation and so you get the shot you need of your subject or of yourself and your subject. If you will be getting only an image of your subject, your chairs should face each other (see Figure 2.1). If you want a *2-shot* (a shot of both of you), your chairs should be angled partially toward each other and placed quite close together so that you get more than a profile of each of your faces, as indicated in Figure 2.2.

- **Put your camcorder or camera on a tripod that is at eye level with your subject.**

People look most natural, and you usually get the most information from the image of their face, if the camera lens is roughly at eye level (as opposed to higher than or lower than the subject).

- **If you want an image of only your subject, place the camera behind you, on either your left or your right.**

To get the most direct shot of your subject's face, the camera must be placed so that it is looking as close to directly at your subject as possible. Because the camera can't comfortably be placed between you and your subject, it needs to be behind you, slightly to your left or your right (see Figure 2.1.) The resulting image will be a three-quarter picture of your subject's face, favoring his right side if the camera is on your left, and vice versa.

- **If you want a shot of yourself and your subject, place the camera so that it is facing both of you, in the center, or favoring either of you.**

Figure 2.2 shows the placement of the camera and chairs for an image that shows each of you about equally. Figure 2.3 shows the placement of the camera and chairs for an image that favors the patient, who is sitting to the left of the camera. Figure 2.4 shows the placement of the camera and chairs for an image that favors you (the health professional) sitting to the right of the camera. (In Figure 2.1 the chairs are across from each other; in Figures 2.2.–2.4 the chairs are at right angles and are usually quite close to each other.) The general principle is, the more of a person's face you capture, the more information you get.

- **Frame the shot.**

If your image is of only your subject (a *single*—only one person in the picture), adjust the *zoom lens* so that you get as much of your subject as you want. Typically, you will want only the subject's head and shoulders (a *medium* shot). If you want a 2-shot, you will need a much wider shot, which includes more than your heads and shoulders.

- **Test the equipment.**

Turn on the recorder and talk to your patient or subject for about 20 seconds. Then play back those 20 seconds to assure that you have the picture and the audio you need.

- **Put the equipment in record mode, return to your seat, and begin the interview.**

Consider beginning the interview with thanking your subject for being willing to be interviewed. If any questions are raised about your subject's consent to the interview, you will have a video record confirming his or her agreement.

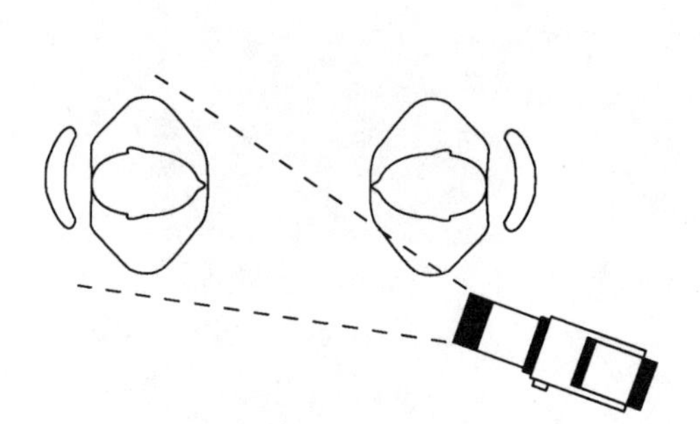

Figure 2.1
Three-quarter shot, subject only.

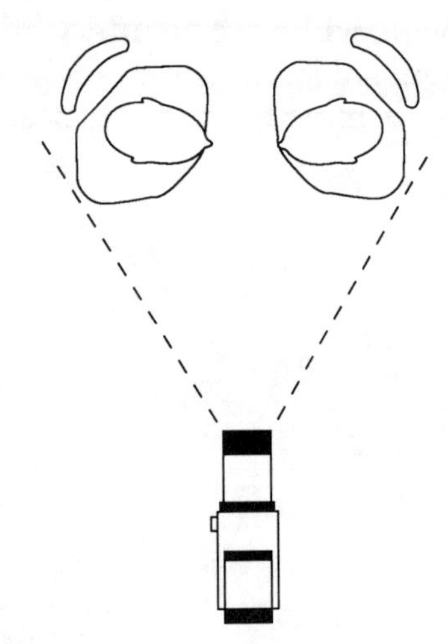

Figure 2.2
Two-shot, balanced.

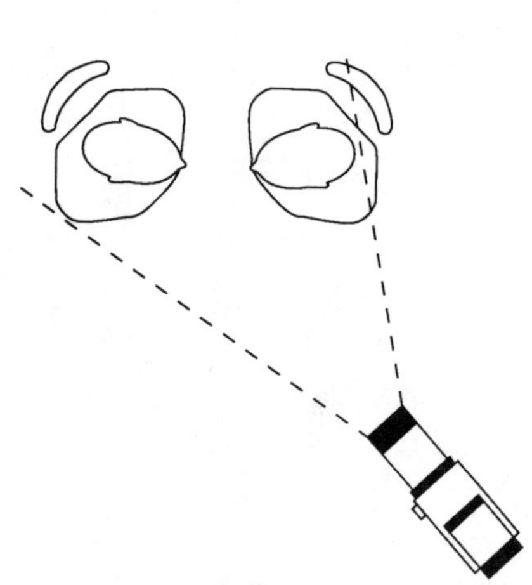

Figure 2.3
Two-shot, favoring patient.

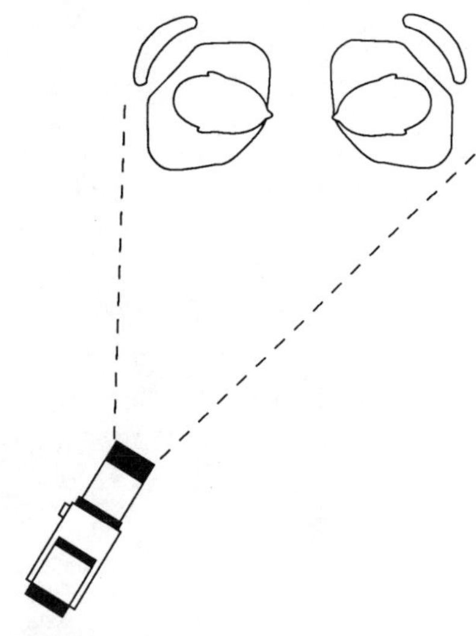

Figure 2.4
Two-shot, favoring interviewer.

Appendix 2.1

Self-Checklist: Preparing for a Videotaped Demonstration

Did I . . .

- ☐ Assess my learners' current capacities for doing the skill I intended to demonstrate?
- ☐ Identify the steps I take when performing the skill as well as the steps beginners need to take—if there is a difference?
- ☐ Talk with learners who have recently mastered the skill, as part of my effort to identify what beginners need?
- ☐ Reflect on the kind of demonstration that will be most helpful to my learners?
- ☐ Identify and make arrangements for the people and resources I need for the demonstration?
- ☐ If real or simulated patients/clients will be involved, prepare them for the demonstration?
- ☐ Arrange for the demonstration to be videotaped and assure that the camera operator knows what the learners need to see and hear?
- ☐ Arrange for needed video equipment?
- ☐ (If my demonstration was taped in a clinical setting.) Ensure that the location was suitable and that personnel at the site were aware of what was happening?

From: Westberg, J., Jason, H. *Teaching Creatively with Video: Fostering Reflection, Communication and Other Clinical Skills,* New York: Springer Publishing Co., 1994.

Appendix 2.2

Self-Checklist: Reviewing a Video Recording with Learners

Did I . . .

- ☐ (If I first did a live demonstration in front of the learners,) invite their questions and comments before playing the tape of that demonstration?
- ☐ Begin by playing the videotape in its entirety, especially if I did not do a live demonstration in front of the learners?
- ☐ Prepare the learners for the review of the tape?
- ☐ Invite the learners to ask me to pause the tape when they had questions or concerns?
- ☐ Pause the tape to discuss what I was thinking during key stages of the demonstration (e.g., my thoughts about the patient's problem)?
- ☐ Pause the tape at key decision points to discuss optional strategies?
- ☐ Pause the tape at key points during the demonstration to discuss what I was feeling (e.g., my feelings toward the patient)?
- ☐ Replay segments of the demonstration multiple times, if appropriate?
- ☐ Review complex, rapid maneuvers and events in slow motion, if appropriate?
- ☐ Invite the learners' questions and comments when I finished reviewing the recording?
- ☐ Provide early opportunities for the learners to practice the new skill, even integrating their practice into the demonstration session so that I could determine whether I needed to provide further demonstrations?

From: Westberg, J., Jason, H. *Teaching Creatively with Video: Fostering Reflection, Communication and Other Clinical Skills,* New York: Springer Publishing Co., 1994.

CHAPTER 3

Selecting and Using Video Triggers

In Chapter 2, we discussed using video clips for illustrating, modeling, and demonstrating. Although we suggested engaging learners by asking them to reflect on questions or issues while watching the video clips, our emphasis was not on stimulating them to respond overtly or immediately, as we try to do when using video triggers.

Video triggers have been defined in a variety of ways. We consider video triggers to be brief video clips that are used for such purposes as provoking reflection, stimulating discussion, helping learners confront their feelings, giving learners practice in responding to challenges, and more. Often video triggers are *vignettes*—brief incidents or scenes. Some educators (e.g., Kagan & Kagan, 1991) create triggers in which a single person looks directly into the camera and makes a statement or asks a question that is intended to evoke a response in the viewer. More typically, triggers created for health professionals are real or dramatized events, often deliberately incomplete, involving interactions between health professionals or learners and their patients/clients or interactions between two or more health professionals. Video clips, such as segments extracted from interviews, films, and documentaries, that were not designed as video triggers, are also used to trigger learners' responses.

When educators use video triggers effectively, they don't simply play the triggers. Rather, before showing a trigger, they typically set the stage and present a challenge to their learners:

> The person you're about to see is coming to the health center for the first time. Imagine he's your patient. What are your initial impressions of him? What additional information do you need to gather so you can help him?

After playing a trigger, the teachers often repeat their challenge and invite their learners' responses.

When using video triggers with small groups, it is usually possible to directly involve all of the learners in the discussion or other activity. But even when working with large groups, it is possible for all of the students to feel engaged, even when only a few students are speaking

In this chapter, we

- identify and discuss reasons for using *video trigger*s in classroom teaching
- identify sources for *video trigger*s and other video clips
- discuss issues that need to be considered when using triggers
- provide suggestions for (1) preparing yourself for using triggers and other video clips and (2) using triggers.

REASONS FOR USING VIDEO TRIGGERS

As we briefly indicated in Chapter 1, video triggers enable you to provide learners with several of the conditions needed for lasting learning. Here we'll give examples of how you can do this, and we'll present some additional reasons for using video triggers when you're teaching in classrooms, conference rooms, and other settings.

You can help your learners understand some of the challenges they face and the capabilities they need.

Many of the tapes produced for education in the health professions capture or depict events that take place in real or simulated health care settings (e.g., a patient who is angry because he had to wait for an hour to be seen, a health professional faced with having to give bad news to a patient, a gravely ill person who wants help with ending her life, a patient who wants to know how much longer he will live). You can also find other video clips that can be used to present challenges (e.g., a segment from a news program in which people discuss how dehumanizing their health care has been). When learners are confronted with real-world events, they can be helped to understand the elements and implications of these challenges and to reflect on the skills they need for dealing with these challenges.

Learners can safely practice complex interpersonal skills.

Video is able to produce a close approximation to human presence (Dowrick & Jesdale, 1991). Because viewers to some degree feel that the people on the monitor are real and present, you can use video to help learners practice their communication skills. The usefulness of video vignettes in teaching interpersonal skills has been confirmed by those who have used them in helping students do such things as recognize cultural issues (Mao, Bullock, Harway, Kjalsa, 1988), relate to elderly patients (Robbins, Fink, Kosecoff, Vivell, & Beck, 1982), and develop skills of empathy and active listening (Sharf & Kahler, 1993).

Before you show a video trigger to learners, you can give them a challenge, such as the following:

> Imagine you're the physician (or nurse, etc.) in this video trigger. When I stop the tape, tell me what you'd say or do next.

Or:

> I'm going to show you a patient (client) who will be speaking directly to you. When I stop the tape, tell me how you'd respond to this person.

When you stop the tape, you could repeat the challenge and invite a number of learners to give their responses aloud (one at a time, of course). As we discuss later, you can even have students role play various continuations of the event with each other.

This use of video triggers enables learners to share and discuss a variety of strategies for handling multiple situations. In the safety of the classroom or conference room, they can improvise and experiment and then get feedback on their efforts. They can literally rehearse a variety of ways of responding to challenging situations, thus building their repertoire of available options for later use.

Learners can practice their observational skills.

Health professionals need to be astute observers of patients and their behaviors. Often they need to pick up important details under the pressure of time. With video triggers you can help learners improve their observational skills. For example, you can show learners 20 or 30 seconds of a health professional interacting with an elderly person who appears depressed and then give the learners the following kinds of challenges:

- Describe the patient you just saw.
- What did you see?
- What did you hear?

Video triggers can help learners recognize and deal with their feelings.

There are a number of strategies for helping learners identify their feelings. You can ask learners to observe an interaction between two or more people (e.g., a nurse talking to a physician) and then reflect on how the interaction made them feel. Prior to showing a trigger you can ask learners to imagine they are one of the people in the trigger (e.g., the nurse, the physician, the mental health professional) and to reflect on how this event might feel in that person's shoes. You might then ask them to view the tape again, now imagining that they are another person in the interaction.

You can also use triggers in which a person (e.g., a patient) looks directly at the viewer and says and/or does something as if communicating directly with the viewer. For example, an angry patient might say, "Do you realize I've been waiting for you for more than an hour!" Again, the setup you offer prior to the viewing of such a trigger is all-important. One approach might be to invite viewers to adopt a role (e.g., a health professional with whom this person had an appointment) and to be open to and to try to verbalize whatever feelings and thoughts emerge in reaction to the patient's statement.

Video triggers can help learners identify their own attitudes and values.

Watching video triggers of people confronting ethical issues, such as whether to have an abortion or whether to discontinue life support, can help learners reflect on and come to grips with their own attitudes and values. For example, you could show your learners a trigger in which an elderly woman in the early stages of Alzheimer's disease asks her doctor to promise her that he will help her end her life before she loses full contact with reality and becomes a burden to her children. You could then pose such questions as:

- How would you feel if you were this patient's physician?
- What would you say?
- What would you do?
- How do you feel about assisting people in their dying?
- What do you think of others who do so?

Some of your learners' responses can enable you to provide them with constructive feedback.

When our learners are silent during a class, we get very little data (mostly nods and facial expressions) about what they are thinking and feeling. Video triggers that provoke overt responses from our learners can give us rich information about them and their learning needs (e.g., about the sophistication of their thinking or their level of sensitivity to interpersonal issues). We can even ask learners to write down their responses and turn them in to us before discussing them. We can then use what we learn from their oral or written responses to guide our instructional efforts and provide them with feedback.

You can capture and hold your learners' attention.

Most learners in the health professions are overwhelmed with obligations. It can be particularly difficult to capture and hold their attention if they just sat through a series of boring lectures, if they have been up all night caring for patients, or if they are in the midst of preparing for an examination. Professional communicators (e.g., public speakers, playwrights, screen writers, and novelists) know the importance of starting with a "grabber"—an attention-getting, even tension-producing statement or juxtaposition of events that attracts the audience and holds their involvement as the story or information they intend to present is developed. As teachers we are also most likely to engage our learners if, at the beginning of a class, seminar, or other educational session, we create a sense that something important will follow. Beginning the session with a provocative video trigger can help you get your learners' attention and quickly convey the message that you and they are embarking on a stimulating event, not a boring lecture.

Most learners can't stay focused on a lecture for more than 15 minutes, and they can become restless even during small-group sessions, so we also need strategies for recapturing or sustaining their interest. During a session, you can use video to provide new energy to a lagging discussion, to offer a change of pace, or to redirect your learners' attention.

You can provide learners with common experiences that stimulate discussion.

Even though some teachers want to involve their learners in lively, meaningful discussions, they find it difficult to get a discussion started, particularly if they are trying to generate a discussion around an abstract issue. Discussions about patient care issues also can be stilted if learners have not yet had clinical experiences of their own on which to draw.

Using a video trigger you can bring reality to an otherwise abstract discussion and simultaneously provide your learners with a shared, provocative experience. For example, rather than having an abstract discussion about impaired health professionals, you could show a vignette in which an apparently impaired health professional is doing a clinical task in a suboptimal, even potentially dangerous fashion. You could invite your learners to react to and discuss the situation portrayed in the vignette and then help the learners extract some general principles and issues from this vignette.

Learners can do in-depth analyses of complex interpersonal interactions.

Some triggers are rich with multiple issues and layers of meaning. You can show learners the same trigger multiple times, each time focusing on different issues. For example, when studying a trigger that depicts a clinician telling a patient that she has a malignant tumor in her breast, you could play the trigger several times, each time giving the learners different challenges. The first time through you might ask your learners to focus on the clinician:

- How would you describe the clinician's approach?
- What impact is his approach likely to have on the patient?

The second time through you might ask your learners to focus on the patient:

- How would you describe the patient's response?
- What hypotheses are you developing about the patient from what you have seen and heard?

The third time through you might turn off the volume and challenge your learners to concentrate on the clinician's and patient's nonverbal communication:

- What are the clinician's nonverbal messages?
- What are the patient's nonverbal messages?
- How do their nonverbal messages compare with their verbal messages?

Learners can become more aware of different perspectives on critical issues.

To provide sensitive, high-quality care, health professionals need to collaborate with patients and their families and among themselves. Typically, different members of the health team have different perspectives on whatever challenge is being addressed. Video triggers enable you to provide learners with opportunities to listen to and weigh the perspectives of others. For example, you could show learners a vignette in which a nurse, physician, and social worker are having difficulty reaching agreement about the care of a patient. When you stop the tape, you could first ask your learners for their overall reactions to the vignette. Then you could interrupt your discussion with your learners and ask three of them to each imagine they are one of the professionals in the vignette and to continue from where the vignette left off.

You can also help learners examine different perspectives by making or using video triggers of patients or others presenting their perspectives on issues you want your learners to reflect upon. (These "person-on-the-street" types of triggers are discussed below.)

Video can bring reality to problem-based learning.

An increasing number of schools in the health professions are using real-world challenges and problems as springboards for learning, rather than waiting until learners have supposedly mastered certain content before giving them opportunities to address real challenges (e.g., Barrows & Tamblyn, 1980; Barrows, 1985; Kaufman, 1985). For example, in their early months of medical school, small groups of students are given problems (typically a patient with a complaint and some critical signs and symptoms) that are designed to help them learn about certain issues, processes, principles, and/or mechanisms. In their attempts to think through and perhaps even solve these problems, students share relevant knowledge and experiences. Usually, they are not expected to understand or solve a problem in a single session. Rather, they identify their "learning issues" (e.g., questions and holes in their knowledge), divide the learning tasks among themselves, engage in individual research and study, report back to the group, and then continue to work on the problem until they understand it or resolve it to their satisfaction. Time is also spent summarizing and integrating what they have learned, including deciding how principles or approaches they have learned might be applied to future problems.

Broadly defined, problem-based learning can also include other educational settings and formats that are built around challenges that learners could face in the real world. For example, an instructor working with a large group can build a presentation or large group discussion around an intriguing problem.

The problems used in problem-based learning are usually introduced in written form. For example, a patient's presenting complaints and perhaps some signs and symptoms are summarized in a few paragraphs. Additional information (e.g., lab findings) may be available in written form later in the discussion in response to the learners' requests. In some situations, learners can also ask to view x-rays and other studies. In large group sessions, instructors sometimes present problems orally.

Video triggers provide an alternative way of introducing challenges to learners that is more lifelike and that can include phenomena that cannot be adequately described on paper (e.g., the patient's affect or the way a patient moves). As with written cases, you can begin with some initial information and then later, in response to a request from the students or at your initiative, provide other information. For example, you could begin a session by showing the first 90 seconds of a visit in which a middle age man complains of headache. You could challenge learners to generate their own issues and learning goals or, if you wanted to begin with a more directive instructional format, you could pose such questions as:

- What are your initial impressions of this patient?
- What else would you like to know about his problem?
- What are some of the different ways in which headaches present?
- What are some structural causes of headache?
- What are some non-structural causes of headache?
- What do you know about the mechanisms of pain?

Later in the discussion you could play one or more short episodes from other parts of the visit, stimulating further discussion. For example, in a second episode the patient might reveal that he is a computer programmer and is under a great deal of stress at work. Now you might ask the learners such questions as:

- Are you entertaining any new hypotheses about the patient's problem?
- What questions would you like to ask this man?
- What do you know about health problems related to computer use?
- What would you look for when you examine him?

After the students have discussed some of the chief issues, you can provoke further reflection and discussion by showing more glimpses of the patient at later points in the interview and examination. You can also have some written information, x-rays, and other materials that you give to students at appropriate times.

SOURCES FOR VIDEO TRIGGERS AND OTHER VIDEO CLIPS

Preproduced Video Triggers

Preproduced video triggers for health professions education (particularly vignettes embedded in longer programs) are available through a variety of sources, such as publishing houses (e.g., Health Sciences Consortium, American Journal of Nursing Company) and societies and associations (e.g., Society of Teachers of Family Medicine, American Psychiatric Association). Video triggers are available for use with students and residents on such topics as communicating with patients, caring for people with HIV and AIDS, caring for depressed people, caring for people from other cultures, elder abuse, depression, women's issues, changing attitudes toward the chronically mentally ill, psychiatric profiles, ethical issues, discharge planning, the nurse-patient relationship, and the nursing process. Video triggers have also been produced for use in faculty development in such areas as clinical teaching in the health professions, the teaching of interpersonal skills, and making presentations. See Appendix 3.1 for some sources of video triggers.

Segments from Video Recordings

Patient interviews and other clinical events. Some schools and programs are beginning to build collections of video recordings of patient-care events, particularly interviews and counseling sessions. If patients have signed appropriate releases for these recordings, you can extract brief segments from the recordings to use as educational triggers.

Home videos. Many teachers have their own video camcorders. If you do, in addition to making recordings in clinical settings, you can make videos in your home or community to illustrate important issues. For example, if you are teaching about child development and have children of your own, you might want to videorecord them as they play or behave in ways you want to illustrate. (Of course, you should secure the informed consent of anyone whose videotaped image you use in your teaching.)

Off-air TV programs. There are a variety of programs on television that can serve as sources of video triggers, including programs explicitly focusing on health care issues, news programs, television movies and sports. Potential vignettes on health-related issues are embedded in situation comedies and television dramas (e.g., *Northern Exposure*). Many of these programs are available for purchase or rental, or they can be recorded off the air. Regardless of the mode of acquisition, keep in mind that virtually all such programs are copyrighted, so you are restricted in how they can be used. Although you may be free under the "fair use" agreement to use them for educational events for which there is no separate charge, you should not make copies or give them to others. If you want to use segments from off-air video programs or motion picture films (see below) as triggers, we recommend that you secure an interpretation of the latest regulations from legal counsel.

Videos of motion picture films. Students often enjoy watching triggers from familiar films. You can use brief segments from films that are explicitly about health care or raise issues pertinent to health professionals (e.g., *Ordinary People, Rain Man, Lorenzo's Oil*, *The Doctor*) or films that deal with other issues you want to illustrate. Alexander, Hall, and Pettice (1994) discuss how they use clips from popular films (or entire films) to teach about psychosocial issues. For example, they use *The Color Purple* and *Nuts* for discussions of child abuse, *On Golden Pond* for discussions of aging, *Kramer vs. Kramer* for divorce and single parenthood, *The Dead Poets' Society* and *The Breakfast Club* for adolescence, *My Left Foot* for disabilities, and *Sleeping with the Enemy* for discussions of spouse abuse. (Note: If you intend to use this source of triggers, please see the note above about legal considerations.)

Video Recordings Made by Learners

An increasing number of learners know how to use simple consumer-level video equipment or can learn the needed skills rather quickly. Using their own equipment or equipment on loan from your institution (if possible), they can make recordings from which video triggers can be extracted. For example, they can interview people who have just had a recent health care visit, asking such questions as:

- How would you describe the care you just received?
- Did you have any concerns that weren't addressed? *If yes*, what got in the way of your problems being addressed?
- Do you have any recommendations on how we can be more effective in responding to your health care needs?

After learners have recorded such interviews, you or they, or both of you, can identify segments that can be used as triggers.

Your Own Creations

As we suggested in the previous chapter, you can create your own video clips. Segments from some of your recordings might be suitable as video triggers. You can also consider producing your own video triggers using actors and/or real learners, professionals, patients, clients, and others. Some of the issues to consider when creating educational videos for health professionals are described by Schoonover, Bassuk, Smith, and Gaskill (1983). (Remember: releases are needed from actors and nonactors.)

ISSUES AND CONSIDERATIONS

The format of the videotapes you use needs to be compatible with the playback equipment.

Videotapes are available in a variety of formats (e.g., VHS, Hi8). Most playback equipment can play tapes of only one format. Some playback equipment can play two related formats. Most schools and programs try to standardize on one or two formats. For example, they might have some equipment that plays the consumer-level VHS tape as well as other equipment that plays professional-level Beta tapes.

As we mentioned in Chapter 1, video equipment can be

grouped loosely into three categories, according to its quality and sophistication (and cost): (1) *consumer*, (2) *educational / industrial,* and (3) *professional.* At this time, four formats dominate the consumer/home market

- VHS (Video Home System) and C-VHS (Compact VHS)
- S-VHS (Super VHS) and C-SVHS (Compact S-VHS)
- 8mm (8-millimeter)
- Hi8 (Hi-band 8-millimeter)

The VHS "family" uses 1/2-inch-wide tapes and includes four members that are fairly closely related: S-VHS equipment can record and play both the higher-quality S-VHS-format and VHS-format tapes. The compact versions of each format are simply smaller quantities of tape in that format, housed in smaller cassettes. (To play a compact tape on regular VHS equipment requires an adapter.) The 8mm family is named for the width of its tape. In parallel fashion, Hi8 equipment can record and play both its own format and that of its lower-quality cousin. Some 8mm equipment can play Hi8 tapes but only at 8mm-quality output.

Many schools still use 3/4-inch or U-matic tape, or an upgraded version known as 3/4 or U-matic SP. (3/4 was once the most widely used professional-level format.) Now many institutions are switching to Betacam (referred to mainly as Beta) and its higher-quality cousin, Beta SP. Both are 1/2-inch tapes.

Internationally, there are additional problems with compatibility.

Tape formats are further affected by local broadcasting conventions. The United States, Canada, and Japan (among others) follow the guidelines of the NTSC (National Television Standards Committee). The British, however, adopted PAL (Phase Alternation Line), and the French and Russians later adopted SECAM (Sequential Couleur a Mémoire). These formats are incompatible with each other, although larger institutions in some parts of the world (few in the United States) have equipment that can switch among NTSC, PAL, and SECAM (Dowrick & Jesdale, 1991). On the horizon at this time is still another format standard, which, when adopted, will provide high-definition television (HDTV).

SUGGESTIONS

PREPARING TO USE TRIGGERS AND OTHER VIDEO CLIPS

- **Review your goals for the session, identifying those best served by video clips, including triggers.**

Whether you are making a presentation or leading a small group session, think through what you want your students or residents to take away from the session and how video might help you achieve these goals. For example, if your goal is for them to better understand the needs of persons with AIDS, you might show them a couple of brief interviews with people who have AIDS. If your goal is for them to practice dealing with patients who are angry, you might show them one or more video triggers depicting people who are angry and challenge them to think through how they would respond to these people.

- **Select appropriate video.**

Above we identified and discussed some sources for video triggers.

- **Secure permission to use triggers, if necessary.**

Above we introduced the copyright and fair use issue. Before using triggers derived from copyrighted materials, ensure that the use you intend to make is appropriate and that needed permissions have been secured.

- **Think through when and how to use triggers and other video clips.**

Consider using video at the beginning of the session to capture the learners' attention. If you are making a presentation, consider using video at different times during your presentation when you anticipate that you will need to change the pace or when you need to change the topic. If you are facilitating a small-group discussion, consider building the entire session around one or more video triggers.

- **Prepare lead-in comments and questions.**

As we've discussed, whether you are giving a presentation or leading a small group, it's usually helpful to set the stage before showing video clips. Particularly when using video triggers it's also important to prepare challenges.

> Mr. Jones came to the health center this morning complaining of chest pain. As we join him, a clinician is examining him. When I stop the tape, think through how you would answer the question Mr. Jones asks.

If you want to use specific lead-ins, consider writing them down. Even consider rehearsing part or all of what you will say.

Try to use open-ended questions and comments. Closed questions usually require simple, short answers and focus on lower levels of thinking, such as the recall of facts.

- How many questions did the nurse ask?
- What were Mr. Garcia's exact words?

Open-ended questions, on the other hand, help learners think broadly about issues. Their answers to open-ended questions give you more clues about their capabilities than do closed questions.

- How would you describe the interaction between the nurse and the doctor?
- How would you approach this patient's problem?

- **If appropriate, plan for mid-playback pauses.**

Some triggers, even very brief ones, are so rich in discussion material that they deserve to be stopped multiple times. Study the triggers you intend to use and identify issues within them that you would like to discuss with your learners. You might well use the same trigger in a variety of ways, depending on your goals and the group's level of readiness.

- **Prepare follow-up questions and comments.**

After showing a trigger, it is usually helpful to repeat the challenge(s).

- What effect is the clinician's approach likely to have on Mr. Jones?
- What would you do as the next step in this exchange?

Once the discussion gets underway, if you want to guide it in a particular direction, some additional specific questions and comments can help. Again, if you have certain questions you want to raise or comments you want to be sure to make, consider writing them down in advance.

- **Devise a strategy for easily accessing each video clip.**

If you plan to use only a few video clips and each one is on a different tape, you can easily access them on their separate tapes by making sure that each tape is clearly labeled and *cued* (set to begin) at the right starting place. The most reliable way to be sure you can find all of the segments you want when you need them is to edit them onto a fresh tape in the sequence you will use them, leaving a few seconds of *black* between each episode. (Blank videotape shows up on a television screen as "snow" or "noise." A *black burst generator* can be used to create a pure black image on the videotape. A lower-quality but acceptable black can be created by running a television camera with its lens cap on while in the record mode.) Note: You are free to make copies of clips onto a new tape only with non-copyrighted material, unless you have secured permission to copy the clips in question.)

Some videocassette recorders provide an *indexing* feature that enables you to insert electronic signals at selected locations on a tape, permitting rapid search for these locations during playback. This feature enables you to use non-contiguous segments from the same tape, but keep in mind that even 20 seconds of waiting while the tape advances to the next index mark can seem too long. If you plan to use the indexing feature, consider engaging the group in a discussion or some other activity while each search is underway. Note: You can only add index marks to tapes that are not "*record-protected*." (All tapes can be—and should be—protected from being accidentally overwritten. As explained in the Glossary, you can override the protection if you want to add an index mark.)

- **Make arrangements for video playback equipment.**

In Chapter 1 we listed the basic equipment you need.

- **Make sure you know how to use the equipment.**

Don't wait until you are in front of your students to learn how to use the equipment. If you don't know how to use the equipment, make arrangements before your session to have someone show you how to use it and then practice using it enough so that it becomes virtually automatic.

- **Check out the room where you will be teaching.**

Make sure there is adequate space for the video equipment and that the room has electrical outlets for the equipment. If you think you will need to turn down the lights to reduce glare on the screen(s) of the monitor(s) or to assure vividness of the projected image, locate the light switches or dimmers that you will need to operate.

USING VIDEO TRIGGERS

- **Before showing a trigger, set the stage and present a challenge.**

If you haven't previously used video triggers with this group, let them know what you plan to do and why. Prior to showing individual triggers, set the stage and present a challenge.

> The video trigger you're about to see is from the film *The Doctor*. The patient in this scene is himself a doctor, but he has just had a throat biopsy because of a growth found after he complained about a persistent cough. In this scene the patient's doctor presents the results of the biopsy. When I stop the tape, I'd like you to describe the doctor's approach and the apparent impact of her approach on the patient and his wife.

You might present another kind of trigger in the following way.

> The other night on television, there was a program on the American public's appraisal of our health care system. Did any of you see it? (Wait for response.) The comments of some of the people interviewed for this program were provocative. I have recorded some excerpts from the program and brought them today. Let's begin with a statement by a schoolteacher who's the mother of two small children. When I stop the tape, I'd like your reaction to her statement.

- **After showing the trigger, repeat the challenge.**

Learners can get so caught up in watching a video trigger that they forget the challenge they have been given, so after showing the trigger, repeat the challenge unless some learners are clearly ready and eager to respond.

- **Avoid telegraphing the "correct" response.**

To stimulate lively discussions, try not to telegraph what you want students to say or feel. Telegraphing is often done through tone of voice and nonverbal communication. It can also be done with leading questions, such as in this unsubtle example: "There was no sign that the nurse was nervous, was there?" And telegraphing can be done with adjectives: "What is your reaction to this seductive patient?"

We are also at risk of telegraphing our views or feelings—and thereby constraining the learners' reactions—by our facial expressions or other nonverbal responses to our learners' initial comments.

- **Consider asking learners to write down their responses.**

Asking learners to commit themselves in writing, before hearing comments from others, can help them get into the desirable habit of reflecting on their thinking and feelings. Having learners write down their responses is an effective strategy for helping all members of a large group be active and involved. Once learners have made their thoughts explicit in this way, they are likely to derive far more from the comments you and their peers make.

- **After asking a question, wait for a response.**

Periods of silence usually feel far longer than they actually are. Many learners are accustomed to teachers who ask and then answers their own questions. Consequently, when you ask a question, they might wait for you to provide your own answer. We encourage you to avoid that trap. Rephrase the question if necessary, but try not to answer it yourself. Waiting just 3–6 seconds is usually enough to convey the seriousness of your intent, and will probably generate a response. (For more on *wait times*, see below.)

- **If you are working with a large group, repeat learners' responses.**

In many auditoriums, it is difficult for members of the audience to hear each other's comments even when people speak loudly. If you are teaching in a large room, it is usually good practice to repeat what learners say, and if necessary, check to make sure you heard them correctly.

- **Pause after a learner responds to your question.**

Rowe (1986) reported that when teachers in her study asked questions of learners, they typically waited only 1 second or less for the learners to reply. And following a learner's response, the teachers waited less than 1 second before reacting to the learner's response or asking their next question. When teachers increased the average length of the pauses at these two key points (after their questions and, even more important, after each student's response) to 3 seconds or more, there were pronounced changes in the students' use of language and logic as well as in student and teacher attitudes and expectations. When teachers waited 3 seconds or more, the following occurred:

- The *length* of student responses increased between 300% and 700%.
- More of the students' inferences were supported by evidence and logical arguments.
- The incidence of speculative thinking increased.
- The number of questions asked by students increased.

- Student-student exchanges increased.
- Failure to respond decreased.
- The variety of students participating voluntarily in discussions increased.

When teachers began using longer wait times on a regular basis, the characteristics of their discourse with students changed. For example, the number and kinds of questions asked by teachers changed. They asked fewer questions, and their questions invited clarification, elaboration, or contrary positions. As teachers succeeded in increasing their average wait times to 3 seconds or more, they became more adept at using student responses, possibly because they too were using the increased time to listen to what students said. In addition, expectations for the performance of certain students seemed to increase. Under the longer wait time schedule, some previously "invisible" students became visible. Teachers made comments such as "He never contributed like that before."

- **React to learners' responses in nonjudgmental ways.**

To facilitate discussions, avoid judging (evaluating) or even giving subtle clues about your reaction to the learners' initial responses. Be friendly but noncommittal as you collect responses from different learners. Verbally or nonverbally, thank learners for their responses but avoid smiling or frowning in ways they might be interpreted as approval or disapproval of what they've said. In addition, refrain from positive or negative statements: "Yes, good response" or "Do you really believe that?" All such subtle and unsubtle judgments from you run the risk of diminishing or canceling the very learner actions you are seeking: the forthright sharing of their thoughts and feelings. When you lose access to that information, you lose your capacity to be fully helpful.

- **Use neutral follow-up questions.**

Nonjudgmental, sequential questioning is also effective in stimulating open, productive group discussions. Your neutral follow-up questions can move learners to deeper levels of thinking. This approach also gives you greater access to your learners' thinking patterns.

Ask a question of one learner. Listen to his or her response and, without betraying your judgment, ask a neutral follow-up question:

- Does anyone have another point of view?
- Any other ideas?

Be sure to use neutral follow-up questions after both acceptable and unacceptable responses from learners so that you do not squelch any interaction by indirectly signaling your judgment. (Note: None of this is meant to suggest that you should be cold or mechanical. You can warmly and genuinely express your delight that the learners are participating, and you should express your appreciation when they take risks, which much of this can involve their doing, all without conveying any judgment about the relative merits of the content of their responses.)

- **Write down the learners' responses.**

Writing summaries of the learners' responses on a chalkboard, flip chart, or overhead transparency gives learners the message that you have heard them. It also provides an opportunity for learners to correct you if you have misheard or misunderstood them.

- **Rotate questions among all learners.**

Teachers tend to appreciate the responses of their more verbal, better-prepared students and can unwittingly direct most of the higher-order questions (questions that challenge learners to analyze or synthesize information rather than merely recalling it) to them (Foster, 1981). In a study of college students, fewer questions were directed at the verbally reticent students (McLeish & Martin, 1975). It can seem wasteful to take time for the responses of learners who seldom have "good" answers. Yet in the hands of teachers who have become effective at asking follow-up questions, any learner's response (or lack of response) can become a stepping-stone to further levels of exploration and learning.

Distributing questions among all members of a group makes an important contribution to everyone's learning. It helps ensure that all learners are alert, engaged, and reflecting on the material at hand. It avoids posturing by some learners, who might begin feeling like favorites, and passivity by others who feel neglected.

- **Discuss the responses.**

Effective teaching does not require remaining perpetually noncommittal. Indeed, it's important for learners to hear and react to your points of view as well as to hear and react to the points of view of others. To create an atmosphere in which you and your learners can have open, honest discussions without their trying to please you, you and they need to work at building and maintaining trust.

- **Be supportive of learners who present views that deviate from the views of the group.**

If the discussions are to be open, honest, and probing, learners need to feel they can take risks, even challenge opinions that are cherished by other group members. When learners take risks, we don't need to support *what* they say. But if learners raise an unpopular question, take an honest stand, or challenge the group (without attacking individual group members), we can commend their courage in doing so and invite a healthy debate.

- **Provide sufficient wait time after questions posed by learners.**

When there is silence following a learner's question, it is tempting, as a group leader, to jump in with a comment or another question. If you can resist this temptation, the group members usually will begin talking. If you cannot resist the temptation, the group members will quickly learn that you will take them off the hook. This can lead them to habitually wait for you to talk after each question you or others ask. If they adopt this passive role, they may not bother to do their own thinking and their learning can be significantly diminished.

- **When a learner asks you a question, turn the question back to the group, at least initially.**

Among the many temptations we need to resist, perhaps the most common—and the most insidious—is the student question that gives us an opportunity to demonstrate our knowledge and judgment. It seems so natural and appealing to simply answer a worthy question. Doing so, unfortunately, can reduce or terminate an important instructional opportunity. As soon as we respond, we remove the possibility of using the learner's question as a diagnostic opening, and we lose access to rich information about the group. We also risk denying the group the opportunity of hearing some responses that may be far closer to what they are ready for than what we would offer.

Consider building into your automatic response repertoire such retorts as:

- Would anyone like to respond to that question?
- Does anyone have any thoughts about the question John just posed?
- That's an important question. We need to spend some time considering various ways it can be answered. Mary, let's start with you.

Although the strategy of turning learners' questions back to the group is likely to be the appropriate approach most of the time, it does not have to be done slavishly. There are times when it is helpful for learners to hear your responses to some of their questions, even before they reflect and respond themselves. Selecting the times for imposing yourself in that way is a judgment call, depending on more variables than we can examine fully here (e.g., the available time, the relevance of the question to the main goals of the session at hand, the likelihood that the questioner's peers will have helpful responses to offer, the sense you have of the group's current level of sophistication in the area of the question, the number of times you have already reflected questions back to the group, and the degree to which you are convinced that what you want to say is likely to be readily understood—and valued—by the group).

- **Replay all or parts of the trigger, as appropriate.**

Many triggers are sufficiently rich to enable fresh insights and reactions with more than one playing.

- **Consider having learners role play extensions of or optional reactions to the event depicted in the trigger.**

Instead of asking learners to indicate what they would have said or done had they been the practitioner in the trigger, you can ask them to convey what they would have said or done through role play with a member of the group or with you.

> John, rather than telling us what you would do, why don't you imagine that Mary is the patient and talk directly to her. And Mary, react to John as if you are the patient.

If other members of the group have ideas about other strategies that might work, consider carrying on with the role playing.

> Mary would you mind continuing to be the patient? Janice, go ahead and ask that question of Mary.

Appendix 3.1

Some Sources of Video Triggers in the Health Professions

American Journal of Nursing Company
555 W 57th Street
New York, NY 10019-2961
800-223-2282

American Psychiatric Association
1400 K St. NW
Washington, DC 20005
202-682-6000

Centre Communications
1800 30th Street, #207
Boulder, CO 80301
800-886-1166

Health Sciences Consortium
201 Silver Cedar Court
Chapel Hill, NC 27514-1651
919-942-8731

Interpersonal Process Recall Institute
University of Houston
425 Farish Hall
Houston, TX 77204
713-749-7621

Society of Teachers of Family Medicine
8880 Ward Parkway
PO Box 8729
Kansas City, MO 64114
800-274-2237

Appendix 3.2

Self-Checklist: Preparing to Use Video Clips

Did I . . .

- ☐ Review my goals, identifying those best served by triggers?
- ☐ Select appropriate video?
- ☐ Secure permission to use the video clips, if necessary?
- ☐ Think through when and how to use each video clip?
- ☐ Prepare “lead-in” comments and questions?
- ☐ Prepare “lead-ins” that are open-ended?
- ☐ Plan for mid-playback pauses, if appropriate?
- ☐ Prepare follow-up questions and comments?
- ☐ Devise a strategy for easily accessing each video clip?
- ☐ Make arrangements for video playback equipment?
- ☐ Make sure I know how to use the equipment?
- ☐ Check out the room where I will be teaching?

From: Westberg, J., Jason, H. *Teaching Creatively with Video: Fostering Reflection, Communication and Other Clinical Skills,* New York: Springer Publishing Co., 1994.

Appendix 3.3

Self-Checklist:
Using Video Triggers

Did I . . .

- ☐ Set the stage and present a challenge before showing each trigger?
- ☐ After showing each trigger, repeat the challenge?
- ☐ Avoid telegraphing the "correct" responses?
- ☐ Consider asking learners to write down their responses?
- ☐ After asking a question, pause and wait for a response?
- ☐ If working with a large group, consider repeating each learner's response?
- ☐ Pause after learners responded to my questions?
- ☐ React to learners' responses in nonjudgmental ways?
- ☐ Use neutral follow-up questions?
- ☐ Write down the learners' responses?
- ☐ Rotate questions among all learners?
- ☐ Discuss the responses?
- ☐ Show support for learners whose views deviate from the norm?
- ☐ Provide sufficient wait time after questions posed by learners?
- ☐ Turn learner's questions addressed to me back to the group, at least initially?
- ☐ Replay all or parts of each trigger, as appropriate?
- ☐ Have learners role play extensions of or optional reactions to the event(s) depicted in each trigger?

From: Westberg, J., Jason, H. *Teaching Creatively with Video: Fostering Reflection, Communication and Other Clinical Skills,* New York: Springer Publishing Co., 1994.

CHAPTER 4

Making and Reviewing Tapes of Role-Played Exercises

Sometimes real clinical encounters cannot provide learners with the opportunities they most need. Some of the practice, especially initial practice, that learners need when developing and refining complex skills cannot or should not take place with real patients/clients. Learning that occurs under simulated conditions—rather than in a real health care setting—can be faster and more effective, while also reducing risks to patients and learners. In simulated situations, learners can safely experiment with alternative approaches. They can find it easier to go through the awkward moments that are often associated with the initial stages of learning; they can immediately discuss with others what they've done; and they can get timely feedback on their efforts.

In classroom settings we can provide some of the experiences our learners need. We can arrange the furniture to simulate the environment that they will need to work in. And we and they can design scenarios that give them the challenges they need. Students who are learning such skills as interviewing or counseling patients can practice them by role playing with a "patient" or "client" who has been scripted to give them the type and level of challenge they need. (The "patient" or "client" can be another student or a stranger hired and trained for the role.) Learners who are refining their skills can role play some of the more challenging interactions for which they need to be prepared, such as giving bad news to family members or dealing with angry patients. Learners can also practice dealing with colleagues, supervisors, and others.

Unlike with real interpersonal interactions, learners who are role playing can repeat an interaction multiple times, experimenting with different strategies. They can take turns working with the same "patient," and they can call for "time out" when they want help from the group. Also, playing the role of patient or family member can give learners insights that will lead them to relate with more sensitivity to real patients, clients, and others.

Taping and then reviewing the recordings of role-played exercises can enhance the learning experience. Seeing themselves on the monitor provides role players with potent feedback. Reviewing the tape allows everyone to examine the interaction with a level of thoroughness and accuracy that isn't possible when the review session must depend on their memory of what happened.

Being videotaped and then reviewing tapes of their performance helps prepare learners for using this instructional strategy in real health care environments. Reviewing each other's work and learning to provide each other with constructive feedback helps prepare learners for video-assisted peer review of encounters with real patients or clients.

In this chapter, we discuss

- reasons for inviting learners to role play
- using simulated patients/clients in role playing
- reasons for taping and then reviewing the recordings of the role-played exercises
- issues and considerations involved in role playing and in reviewing recordings of role-played exercises

and we provide suggestions for

- preparing for a session in which you will invite your learners to role play and then review recordings of their role playing
- training simulated patients
- preparing learners for their first role playing and review session
- reviewing the recordings of the taped exercises.

REASONS FOR LEARNERS TO ROLE PLAY

As we discussed in Chapter 1, very little meaningful, lasting learning of complex capabilities occurs without considerable practice. However, unsupervised trial-and-error practice can be inefficient, can lead to the solidification of bad habits, and can be hurtful to patients and learners.

As soon as possible, beginners need to experience some of the career challenges they will face.

Learners are most likely to work hard at acquiring knowledge and capabilities if they are clear about the challenges they will face in their careers and the ways in which the knowledge and capabilities you are offering will help them meet those challenges. The sooner our learners are confronted with real-world challenges, the sooner they are likely to become active participants in their education.

Without prior preparation through supervised, simulated practice, some patient care demands can cause learners unnecessary discomfort or embarrassment.

When unprepared learners are pushed prematurely to use new skills with real patients, they can experience high levels of stress from knowing they are not ready for this challenge. If learners experience difficulties when using new skills with patients, they can suffer unnecessary discomfort and embarrassment. As a self-protective adaptation, they may even suffer long-term negative consequences, such as avoiding the further practice and use of the skill they were trying to learn, resisting efforts to learn other new skills, and perhaps becoming indifferent to their own feelings, their patients' feelings, or both.

When practicing new, complex skills or changing established behaviors, learners often pass through a stage of feeling "functionally grotesque."

When working with adults who want to make significant changes in their skiing technique, instructors at a prominent Colorado ski school warn these learners that they must prepare themselves for a difficult phase in which they will feel "functionally grotesque." These instructors correctly point out that the process of developing new behaviors or changing customary patterns requires substantial practice of the alternative patterns. During the early stages of this practice we tend to feel awkward, uncomfortable, and grossly incompetent. Many people who are experiencing the side effects of significant learning describe themselves as feeling "lousy," "like I've deteriorated," "like I'm a little child again." The sense of stumbling clumsiness and incompetence is genuinely unpleasant and embarrassing for many people. Whether learning a new sport, how to use a computer, how to play a musical instrument, or some new clinical skill, few adults escape these unpleasant feelings if they are making a genuine effort to change.

Whenever we want students or residents to learn new capabilities, especially ones that require modifying deep-seated habits—such as their ways of relating to patients or thinking through problems—we need to warn them that from time to time they may feel functionally grotesque. Knowing that their teachers expect and accept their being temporarily less than polished helps many learners tolerate the unpleasantness.

The practice of most complex skills requires support, and practice should begin in a "safe setting."

For learners to take the risks involved in complex learning, they need to feel that they are in a setting where they can safely make mistakes, where they can go through the inevitable periods of feeling functionally grotesque without the fear of being hurtful to patients or of embarrassing themselves in front of patients and staff. They need to know they are in an environment where it is anticipated and accepted that they will make mistakes and will get help in learning from those mistakes.

Initially, you can simplify the learners' challenges.

Learning some new skills can demand more than learners are ready to handle; it can be overwhelming. In the classroom you can help learners reduce or avoid the discouragement that accompanies excessive challenges by temporarily simplifying their learning tasks.

You can have learners work on a segment of an interaction rather than the entire interaction. For example, if you want your students to learn strategies for helping patients stop smoking, you could have them role play only the data-gathering component of the interaction (e.g., finding out how the patient feels about his smoking and what he's already done, if anything, to stop smoking) rather than the entire counseling session. Or if they are learning to take a history or do an assessment, you could have them role play only the first 5 minutes of those interactions.

You can also have them focus on a single skill in an interaction that calls for multiple skills. For example, if you want them to learn to be more open-ended when gathering information, you could have them role play a scenario and concentrate only on trying to be open-ended. In addition, with role playing you can simplify your learners' challenges by such modifications as giving them more time than they would have in real patient care settings and designing the patient roles so that the "patients" have only one problem and are cooperative.

As they are ready, you can increase the learners' challenges.

There are a variety of ways in which you can increase your learners' challenges. You can have them move from doing part of an interaction to doing an entire interaction, from practicing a component of a skill to practicing the entire skill, from practicing a single skill to practicing multiple skills at once. You can also provide real-world distractions (e.g., having a phone ring) or pressure (e.g., being told that other patients are waiting and they have to hurry up).

Learners can request certain challenges.

You can invite learners to identify tough situations that they would like help learning to deal with and then design a scenario that gives them the challenges they want. For example, if a learner has difficulty working with patients who are demanding, you can develop a role-play situation in which the learner interacts with a "patient" who makes a series of demands.

You can give learners experience with challenges that may not be routinely available during their clinical experiences in your program.

As we've discussed, when precepting learners in health care settings, we can't always be certain they will have the experiences we or they feel they should have. If, for example, there are virtually no people infected with HIV served by your clinical facility, your learners could fail to get some experiences they may need in caring for people with HIV in the future. With role playing, you can give them a taste of some of the challenges that may be infrequent in your setting but that they need as part of preparing for their careers.

Learners can experiment with optional ways of behaving.

When working with real patients, it can be difficult and even unwise to experiment with a variety of strategies. And it isn't possible to repeat an encounter several times, each time trying a different approach. In the safety of the classroom, though, learners can try out different ways of relating to patients and others, and they can repeat an encounter. For example, learners who feel they are too passive can practice being more assertive. Or a learner can try different ways of relating to the same "patient" and then, during the review session, examine the impact each of these behaviors had on the patient.

Learners can comfortably ask for assistance during an interaction.

You can offer learners the option of declaring "time out" during a session so that they can request assistance from you or their peers.

USING SIMULATED PATIENTS/CLIENTS

Simulated patients or clients are people who have been trained to play a particular role. Typically, they are prepared to present with a certain problem or situation. They have information (e.g., their symptoms, relevant historical information, and pertinent issues in their lives) that they provide to the learner if she or he communicates effectively with them. Sometimes simulated patients or clients present an additional level of challenge by initially being difficult to work with (e.g., angry, demanding, withdrawn). Then, if the learner is skillful in working with them, they moderate their stance.

If you want someone who can play a particularly difficult role, you may want to recruit and train an actor. Otherwise there are many potential sources for simulated patients: retired people, patients from your practice who can play themselves or someone else, members of your administrative staff who want to participate in the educational program.

The following are some arguments to consider when deciding whether to use simulated patients in addition to or instead of having learners play the roles of patients or clients.

They can add more realism to the interaction.

Some learners, especially those who are new to role playing, can find it easier to relate to a simulated patient than to a peer in the role of patient. Imagining that a stranger is their patient can be easier than trying to imagine that their peer (friend) is some other person who is seeking care from them.

You can have wider latitude in designing patient roles.

Some groups of learners can be rather homogeneous. When you select and train simulated patients, you can include people and roles involving age groups, cultural and socioeconomic backgrounds, and issues that are not represented among your learners.

You can design more complex patient roles.

If properly prepared, competent actors can portray a wide range of people and conditions and can reliably remain in character. Even some nonactors can portray complex patients, particularly if the role is not a great stretch for them.

You can give several learners the same challenge, enabling you and them to study the parallels and differences among the encounters.

People trained to present in the same way and to reliably provide the same information are usually referred to as *standardized patients*. If these simulators are not excessively standardized, if they have been prepared to adapt to a range of different approaches, as do real patients, they can provide some highly instructive contrasts. Having several students role play with the same patient can allow learners to see how potentially similar encounters can differ when handled by people who use different approaches, have different personal styles, or have varying levels of competence. Reviewing video recordings of these encounters side by side can give you and your learners instructive comparative information.

You can train them to provide helpful feedback.

Effectively prepared simulated patients (see later in this chapter, under "Training Simulated Patients") can make important contributions as providers of feedback to the learners with whom they work. Once they understand and can use the principles of constructive feedback, they can provide immediate, credible, helpful observations on how they felt and behaved during their clinical encounter with learners.

REASONS FOR TAPING AND REVIEWING RECORDINGS OF ROLE PLAYS

Learners who are new to being videotaped and reviewing their recordings can practice these activities in a safe setting.

We have repeatedly found that learners whose initial experiences with being videotaped and with reviewing their recordings are in safe classroom settings have little trouble later being videotaped with real patients. They are also better prepared for reviewing the recordings of their interactions with real patients.

Learners can practice providing feedback and other help to each other.

In Chapter 7 we discuss the strategy of having peers jointly review video recordings of their real patient encounters and give feedback to each other. Providing feedback to each other about simulated patient encounters can prepare learners for giving feedback to each other regarding their efforts in real patient encounters and can help them be effective teachers of patients and others in the future.

Students can learn to use video equipment.

Ultimately, it is desirable for learners to participate in taping themselves and other learners in patient care settings. If they learn how to use the equipment in the classroom, they will be prepared to make recordings or help make recordings in other settings.

Video playbacks of their performance can provide learners with potent feedback about their efforts.

Sports coaches have long recognized the usefulness of having athletes review recordings of their performance (McCallum, 1987; Rothstein, 1981). Those of us who have been videotaped while teaching, caring for patients, or learning a new sport and then reviewed these recordings with teachers or coaches can attest to the power of such experiences. Teachers and coaches can tell us what we did and how we looked and sounded but that seldom has the impact of seeing it for ourselves through video recordings.

Learners can reflect on optimal strategies available at decision points.

Throughout our professional work, as researchers and as clinicians, we are dealing with decision points: those moments when our tasks involve recognizing that a branch point has been reached and that a selection needs to be made among available options. Video recordings of role plays of clinical interactions can help learners identify key decision points, reflect on the options open to them, and the reasons for the choices they made.

Reviewing recordings can prompt learners to reflect on their internal processes during role-played events.

As Kagan and colleagues have demonstrated (Kagan & Kagan, 1991; Kagan & Krathwohl, 1967), reviewing video recordings of events in which they participate prompts learners to remember what they were thinking and feeling during the event. Recalling these thoughts and feelings allows us and them to reflect on and assess their internal processes (more on this in Chapter 6).

Learners can study their nonverbal behavior.

The nonverbal messages that health professionals give to patients and others can impact greatly on the care they provide. Yet most learners—even seasoned professionals—have few occasions in which they get feedback about their nonverbal behavior. When reviewing video recordings of themselves, learners can study their facial expressions, body language, and gestures, reflecting on the meaning of these elements of communication and on the impact they might have on patients and others.

Learners can reflect on the experience of being a patient.

Some learners in the health professions have had little experience with being a patient and don't fully appreciate what it can be like to be ill and feel vulnerable. And they might not appreciate the impact that a physician, nurse, or other health professional can have on a patient. Playing the role of patient and then reviewing a recording of the role play can help learners recognize some of the issues facing patients and some of the ways they can be most helpful to patients.

Learners can study the recordings further after class.

It is often difficult to extract all of the learning possibilities from a recording during class. If all of the people who appear on a recording consent to allow the learner to study the recording out of class (i.e., alone or with a peer), the student may be able to learn even more from the role-play experience.

ISSUES AND CONSIDERATIONS

Initially, some learners may be uncomfortable with role playing and reviewing recordings of role-played events.

Learners who are new to role playing patient care interactions are likely, at least initially, to feel functionally grotesque. Particularly if learners have had hurtful experiences with role playing or with reviewing recordings of themselves, they may feel uneasy about doing so again. Shortly, we provide suggestions for assessing their level of readiness and for taking steps to help them feel more comfortable.

Some learners may contend that role playing is "phony."

Not uncommonly, some learners resist role playing, particularly with other students, saying that it bears no relationship to real life. If you sense that some of your learners feel this way, you might talk with them about how all of us do some role playing when first learning new skills and assuming new ways of being. Until new skills have become a routine part of us, we are playing a role.

Most role-played events should be simple and should focus on process rather than content.

Memorizing information and trying to learn lines can distract learners from the value of role playing. As we discuss below, you usually need to give learners some basic information about their roles, but if they are trying to remember specific information or lines, they are likely to feel artificial and not identify with their role. The learning that comes from role playing usually comes from reflecting on *how* learners interacted with others (process) rather than from whether the details of the interaction were fully accurate (content).

Most role-played events should be brief so that there is sufficient time to review them and learn from them.

In a 50- or 60-minute instructional session, there may be time to do and review only one role-played event. Before the role play, time needs to be allowed for setting up the room and the equipment and preparing the learners for the role play and review. In the hands of an effective teacher, it can take at least 20 minutes to review and discuss a 5-minute role-played event.

SUGGESTIONS

MAKING GENERAL PREPARATIONS

- **Identify the capabilities your learners need to develop that can best be learned at certain stages by role playing.**

Role playing with video review can contribute at several stages in the learning of complex skills, such as interviewing and counseling. With modification of the goals and the assigned roles, role playing can be helpful during initial practice as well as later when learners are refining their capabilities and learning more sophisticated approaches.

- **Identify the events you want your learners to role play.**

Think through some events, preferably short ones, in which the learners need to use the capabilities they are to develop. Identify the characters involved in the event (e.g., a learner and patient). Keep in mind that for every 5 minutes of role-play you need to allow 10–20 minutes for review and critique.

- **Develop brief "scripts" for the role players.**

Typically, learners who are in the provider role are asked to be themselves and are given instructions that include

- whom they will be interacting with (e.g., the person's name and other information they would normally get in the situation being simulated)
- the circumstances under which they will be encountering each other
- their tasks.

Patients' (clients') scripts can include the following kinds of information:

- pertinent information about who they are (e.g., age, family and work situation, life style)
- the nature and history of their problem

- what if anything they have done to care for themselves
- other information (e.g., associated health problems, relevant family history)
- where and under what circumstance they will be encountering the learner (e.g., a first visit to a health center)
- their emotional state when they first meet with the learner (e.g., sad, angry).

Often "patients" are asked to ad-lib information that is not in the script.

When developing patient/client scripts or scripts of other characters (e.g., family members) for learners or other nonactors, consider making these characters somewhat similar to the age and socioeconomic characteristics of the role players. Try to develop patient problems that are largely invisible except for facial expressions and gestures (e.g., a headache or stomach pain) as opposed to highly visible problems (e.g., a laceration on the patient's face). Select simple common problems that the learners or other nonactors might have had themselves or experienced with friends or family members. Keep scripts as simple as possible, particularly if they will be used by learners who won't have much time to review them or prepare prior to role playing.

- **Make arrangements for the video-recording and playback equipment.**

The equipment you'll need includes

- a monitor (or multiple monitors, or a video projector and screen, if you're working with a large group)
- a camera and recorder or a camcorder
- the camcorder you used for recording, or a separate unit for playing back the tapes
- blank tapes that can be used for recording the role-played events
- a remote control
- a cart for the equipment, preferably with wheels
- a high enough surface on which to place the monitor for the learners to see it clearly (the top shelf of most video carts can serve this purpose).

- **Be sure you know how to use the equipment.**

Practice using the equipment in advance of the class if necessary.

- **Think through how you will arrange the room.**

For many role plays the only props you need are two chairs facing each other in such a way that the subjects can easily talk to each other and their faces can be seen by the television camera. If you are working with a small group of learners, they can be seated in a semicircle around the role players. During the role play, there should be space for the camera operator to get a clear picture of the role players. (See Figures 2.1–2.4 for examples of ways that the camera and the chairs of the role players can be arranged.)

During the review of the video recording, the monitor can be rolled into the center of the semicircle where everyone can see it. If the focus of the review session will be the learner who played the key role (e.g., provider), he or she can sit near the monitor.

- **Prior to the class session, consider getting commitments from some learners that they will role play during class.**

Getting learners to volunteer to do the first role-play exercise can be challenging. If the first role play goes well, other learners usually are more comfortable volunteering to do subsequent role plays. If you anticipate that you might have difficulty getting volunteers during class, consider approaching some learners prior to class and securing their commitment in advance.

- **Consider inviting some students to learn how to operate the video equipment so that they can help with the production.**

Having two or more learners who can operate the video equipment can relieve you of that responsibility so that you can focus on the learners and the role playing. Asking potentially shy people to operate the equipment can be a way of initially helping them to feel that they are part of the production without being “onstage.” Eventually, they should also take their turns in front of the camera.

TRAINING SIMULATED PATIENTS

- **Recruit and select people to be trained as simulated patients.**

If you are at an institution that regularly uses simulated or standardized patients, you can probably draw on these patients, even ask them to play some of the roles they have been taught. If you need to recruit new people, consider getting experienced actors who have had training in assuming roles and taking direction. Or as we suggested earlier, recruit patients from your practice, administrative people in your program, or others from the community. Avoid people who have personal agendas that might interfere with the review process, such as unresolved personal or medical problems they want to address.

- **Give scripts to the actors.**

See above for suggestions about what should be in the scripts.

- **Consider showing the actors video recordings of real or simulated patients who have the characteristics you want them to portray.**

Consider building a library of video recordings of real or simulated patients who illustrate characteristics and behaviors with which you want learners to be familiar. If you intend to show these recordings to actors (or learners), be sure you have the written informed consents of those who appear in the recordings.

- **Demonstrate characteristics that are difficult to describe.**

If you want an actor to assume particular characteristics, such as a particular gait or affect, but don't have video recordings that illustrate these characteristics, consider demonstrating them to the actor yourself or having someone else do so.

- **Rehearse each actor.**

Find a colleague or other person who can play the role of a typical learner who will be working with the simulated patients. Ask this person to assume the role of learner and carry out the activity (e.g., interview or examine the patient) that the real learners will be asked to do. (You can also ask a real learner who has had experience working with simulated patients to be the learner.) After the role play, give the simulated patient feedback on his or her performance. If possible, give the patient practice working with people who portray a variety of different kinds of learners. Also, if possible, use video recording and playback.

The extent to which you need to rehearse simulated patients depends on such factors as the complexity of the case, the extent to which it is important for the patient to initially present in a predictable, consistent way with each learner, and the purpose of the videotaped patient encounter (whether the role play is for the learners' informal practice or if it is part of a formal evaluation process). Another factor that can contribute to the amount you want to invest in a particular simulated patient is the extent to which you will be using this person in future sessions.

- **Introduce the simulated patients to any evaluation forms they will need to complete about each learner.**

Be sure the actors understand all of the items on the form. Consider having them complete the form after they rehearse an encounter. Then review and discuss what they have done.

- **Describe and discuss the review process.**

Describe what will happen during the review process. If there are some particular ways you want simulated patients to provide feedback, consider demonstrating these strategies and/or showing the actors video recordings of real or simulated patients using these strategies.

- **Rehearse the actors in their roles as providers of feedback.**

When an actor rehearses his or her patient role with a "learner," videotape this encounter. Then invite the actor and the "learner" to review the video recording using whatever format will be used in the review sessions. Whenever it's appropriate, stop the action, discuss what is happening, give the actor feedback on what he or she is doing, and provide any needed direction. After the actor has practiced giving feedback to a typical cooperative learner, consider having the "learner" take on the characteristics of a more challenging learner (e.g., one who is highly defensive or self-deprecating) and again rehearse the review session.

For more on preparing standardized patients, see Barrows (1987).

PREPARING LEARNERS FOR THE FIRST ROLE PLAYING AND REVIEW SESSION

Most of the following suggestions pertain to steps to take the first time your learners role play and review recordings of these events. At subsequent sessions, you can go more directly into role playing. The steps below, which pertain to assessing the learners' experiences with role playing, being videotaped, and reviewing their recordings, might best be taken in a class session that occurs before the session in which the learners first role play. If you know about your learners' experiences prior to the role playing, you can use this information to design the role-playing session so that it is congruent with their levels of readiness.

- **Assess your learners' experiences with role playing.**

Information about whether your learners have already had role playing experience and how they feel about the experiences they've had can guide you in introducing the role-playing exercises, choosing a learner for the initial role playing, and determining the complexity of the roles you assign learners to play.

- **Assess your learners' prior experiences with being videotaped and seeing themselves on television.**

With the wide use of consumer video-recording equipment, most or even all of your learners are likely to have seen themselves on television. If some of your learners have not been videotaped, it can be useful to find out if their having not been taped is due to their discomfort with the process. If they are uncomfortable, you may need to take special measures to help them become comfortable with the process.

- **Assess your learners' prior experiences and levels of comfort with using video for reviewing the practice of new skills.**

While learning a sport or some other skill, some of your students may have worked with coaches in reviewing video recordings of themselves engaged in the sport or skill they were developing. Others might have already reviewed videotapes of their clinical work. Find out if any of them have had such experiences and, if so, how those experiences were for them.

If they have had good experiences, you and they are fortunate. If they had hurtful experiences, we recommend finding out what went wrong and what you can do to help them gain some trust in you and the process. Learners who have had negative experiences often report that their teachers or coaches put them down or embarrassed them in front of others. Also, some learners have been pushed prematurely into excessively demanding challenges. As we explain shortly, there are ways to overcome such negative experiences.

- **Ensure that your learners understand the value of role playing and the review of recordings.**

Most of us don't get maximum benefit out of experiences we don't value. If you suspect that some of your learners do not understand the value of role playing and the review of recordings, take time to understand what might be the basis for the way they regard these activities. Try to help them value these activities, perhaps by sharing your own experiences.

- **If your learners are uncomfortable with videotaping, consider doing something light for a short while to put them at ease.**

If you are working with a small group of learners, you can break the ice by using the video camera for a brief diversion before getting down to more serious business. You can videotape all of them as they arrive for the session and talk with you and each other. Then play back the tape so that they all have the experience of seeing themselves. Or let students take turns videotaping you and each other and then review the tape.

- **Ensure that everyone understands how the role playing and the review of the tape will be done and what will happen to the tape(s) after the session.**

Tell the learners if there will be a time limit on their role plays. Typically in classroom teaching, role plays are limited to 3–5 minutes and are stopped before the interaction reaches its natural conclusion. Learners are told not to worry about time and to let the events unfold at a natural pace. (Remember to keep track of the time and call an end to the role play.)

You can wait until just before the review of the tape to give learners the details about how the review will be done. Some learners worry that the tape will be played to others after class. Be sure to let them know what will be done with the tape, assuring them (if it's true) that their privacy will not be violated. (Sometimes the learners who have the key roles in role play exercises borrow or keep their tapes for their own review. Sometimes the recording is erased immediately after class.)

- **Ask for one or more volunteers to do the role playing, unless you made arrangements with some learners before class.**

Give the script(s) to the learner(s) to study for a few minutes.

- **Set the stage.**

Introduce the event to be role played (e.g., "Susan will be interviewing a patient who has come to the clinic with a complaint of headache" or "Tom has been asked to meet with a patient who thinks she would like to stop smoking"). If you have not already done so, literally set the stage by arranging the furniture. Consider having learners who are anxious about role playing or being taped help you with this task to help put them at ease and to involve them in the "production."

- **Set up the camera so that you get the picture(s) you need.**

Some students who won't be role playing can sit or stand in for the role players while you or a learner frames the picture. (This gives the role players time to study their scripts and get into their roles.)

If the role players will be in one place throughout the encounter (e.g., sitting in chairs), you can frame the picture so that it includes both people (a *2-shot*). Then, once you start the recording, if you are satisfied with having a *static* shot (e.g., the same picture of the two people), you can leave the picture as it is, unless your subjects move out of the frame. Usually, the camera should be placed in front of and in between your subjects so you can see about three-quarters of each of their faces (see Figure 2.2).

If you want to see more of the "patient's" face, you'll need to move the camera in the direction of the learner and shoot somewhat over the learner's shoulder (see Figure 2.3). You'll need to do the reverse if you want to see the learner's full face (see Figure 2.4). The decision about where you place the camera depends on the information you want. For example, if you want the learners to study the "patient," you will need to arrange for the camera to see more of the "patient's" face.

- **Test the equipment.**

It is disheartening to start a playback session and discover that you have no picture or no sound or that your camera was accidentally moved so that all you have are pictures of your subjects' feet. To ensure that you get what you need, before doing the actual recording let your subjects know you will test the equipment. Ask them to talk to each other in the tone of voice they anticipate using during the recorded interaction. Record them for 10 to 20 seconds and then replay the recording, checking the framing, quality of the picture and the sound. If all looks good, go ahead with the recording. If not, make needed adjustments.

- **If you are operating the camera, avoid excessive and rapid movements.**

Jerky and excessive movements can distract viewers from the real purpose of the recording. If you are operating the camera, avoid excessive *pans* (side-to-side movements) and *zooms* (changing close-ups to long shots or vice versa). When you need to change shots, make your changes slowly and smoothly. If you haven't done so before, a little advance practice doing slow camera moves can significantly improve the quality of your recording.

- **If you want learners to analyze the recording, avoid directing the learners' attention with the camera.**

If you are operating the camera, it is tempting to *direct* the shots; that is, to make decisions about what the viewer will see and focus on, such as the patient's nervous hand mannerisms. If the videotapes are being created so that learners can critique their own performance, it is usually best to stay on a static shot that includes all of the major action. That way, the learners can make their own discoveries about anything significant that was happening during the encounter, without any influence from in-camera editing.

- **While you are taping, turn off the monitor so that learners aren't diverted.**

If for some reason you need to keep the monitor on, turn it so that the role players and even the other learners can't see it.

- **Stop the taping after the allotted time.**

You might allow some slippage if interesting things are happening, but ensure that there is sufficient time for the review.

REVIEWING THE VIDEO RECORDINGS

The steps to take in reviewing the tape depend on the nature of the role play, the purpose of the review session, and whether a simulated patient will participate in the review. If you will be inviting each learner to do a self-critique and encouraging learners to give feedback to each other, you need to assess their prior experience with doing these things and provide guidance, as needed, particularly in giving constructive feedback. (See Chapter 6 for a discussion of facilitating learners' self-critique. See Chapter 8 [including Appendix 8.3] for a discussion of preparing learners to give feedback to each other. Also, see Chapter 9 for suggestions about reviewing recordings with simulated patients.)

- **Discuss the format for the review session, including any ground rules.**

The format will vary depending on what you are trying to accomplish. One strategy is to focus primarily on the learner who played the key role. In Chapter 8, in our discussion of peer review, we propose a format for doing that (see Appendix 8.4). In this chapter we propose another format: having the key role player serve as a proxy for the other learners and focusing more on what everyone can learn from the role play than on the key role player's performance. Ground rules for the review of all recordings should include being supportive of each other and providing feedback and suggestions in constructive, not hurtful ways.

- **First invite the learner(s) involved in the role playing (particularly those in key high-risk roles) to reflect on the interaction.**

If one person was in the key role, invite that person to take the lead with such steps as reflecting on how it felt to be in that role, what she thought she did well, what she had difficulty with, and what she wants to address in the review session. Also invite others who did role playing to reflect on these or other issues that you identify.

- **Consider inviting the learner in the key role to handle the remote control.**

Having the key learner control the playback has both symbolic and practical value. Symbolically, this gesture indicates that learners are active partners in the teaching-learning process and that their learning is literally in their hands. From a practical standpoint, doing so can help learners gain comfort in operating the video equipment, thereby making it easier for them to use the equipment by themselves for private self-critique of their patient interactions and with others for peer reviews. Finally, the more active that learners are in all aspects of using the video process, the more likely they are to begin regarding it as an integral part of their current and future learning.

- **If time is limited, decide which part(s) of the tape to review.**

As mentioned earlier, a reasonably thorough approach to reviewing tapes tends to require about 3–5 minutes of review time for each minute of recording. Keep track of the recording process so that you know how long the tape is. Try to determine the most desirable ratio of review time to tape time for your purposes so that you can decide in advance how long the role play should be and how much of the recording you and the learners can review.

- **Invite the learners to identify the decision points in the role-played interaction, including the available options.**

Most complex human interactions have multiple decision points. Discuss this concept with the learners and invite them to identify where the decision points are in the role-played interaction by signaling for the playback to be paused at each of those points. Initially, you may have to help the learners recognize when decision points occur.

Invite a discussion of what occurred in the role play at each decision point. Before giving others a chance to talk, invite the key learner to describe and assess what he did. Also, consider giving the key learner the first chance to propose other options that might have been available at each point. If appropriate, you might want to invite learners to briefly role play some of the options that are discussed.

- **If any learners break the ground rules, temporarily stop the review process.**

Learners who are members of well-established small groups can learn to regulate their group process, particularly if they are initially helped to do so. If a member of such a group breaks a rule, someone in the group may well intervene. In some groups, however, especially those that are newly established, you may need to intervene when something goes wrong.

Let's say that a group you are facilitating decided they will not use demeaning language when giving feedback to each other, but one of the students just turned to the designated learner and said, "That was a really stupid thing to do." If group members are committed to the ground rule of not using demeaning language, all you might need to do is say, "Let's stop for a moment." Just doing that might cause the student who made the remark to apologize. Or another group member might draw attention to what happened. However, if no one picks up on your concern, you could be more specific: "What just happened?" If the group still doesn't respond, you might need to address the issue directly.

Be sure that all members of your group understand your concern before proceeding with the review session. If you don't take this step, the designated learner might be hesitant to be optimally candid, fearing that something else he says could lead to additional hurtful remarks by a member of the group.

- **At the end of the review session, give learners an opportunity to summarize what they have learned as well as issues they want to explore.**

First invite the key role player and the other role players to summarize what they learned from the role play and the video-assisted discussion. Then invite the other learners to do likewise. Where possible, try to pull together and highlight key issues and principles. Also invite the learners to identify issues they want to learn more about and skills they want to practice in the future. Even have them suggest role plays that can be done at future sessions.

ADDITIONAL READINGS

van Ments, M. (1983). The effective use of role-play: A handbook for teachers and trainers. London: Kogan Page Ltd.

Milroy, E. (1982). Role play: A practical guide. Aberdeen: Aberdeen University Press.

Appendix 4.1

Self-Checklist: Preparing Learners for and Doing the Initial Videotaped Role Play

Did I . . .

- ☐ Explore and assess the learners' prior experiences with role playing?
- ☐ Explore and assess the learners' experiences with being videotaped and seeing themselves on television?
- ☐ Explore and assess the learners' experiences and comfort with using video for reviewing the practice of new skills?
- ☐ Ensure that the learners understood the value of role playing and the review of recordings?
- ☐ If the learners were uncomfortable with videotaping, do something to put them at ease?
- ☐ Ensure that the learners understood how the role playing and the review of the tape would be done?
- ☐ Ask for volunteers to do the role playing?
- ☐ Set the stage and arrange the room?
- ☐ Set up the camera so that we got the picture(s) we needed?
- ☐ Test the equipment before recording the role playing?
- ☐ Avoid excessive and rapid camera movements?
- ☐ Avoid directing the learners' attention with the camera?
- ☐ During the taping, turn off the monitor so that the role players and other learners were not diverted?
- ☐ Stop the taping after the allotted time?

From: Westberg, J., Jason, H. *Teaching Creatively with Video: Fostering Reflection, Communication and Other Clinical Skills,* New York: Springer Publishing Co., 1994.

Appendix 4.2

Self-Checklist: Reviewing the Recording

Did I . . .

- ☐ Discuss the format for the review session, including any ground rules?
- ☐ Ensure that learners knew how to provide constructive feedback to each other (see Chapter 8)?
- ☐ First invite the learner(s) involved in the role playing (particularly those in key high-risk roles) to reflect on the interaction?
- ☐ Invite the learner in the key role to handle the remote control?
- ☐ If time was limited, decide which parts of the tape to review?
- ☐ Invite learners to identify the decision points and pause the tape at those places?
- ☐ Invite the key role players to discuss what occurred at the decision points and then invite the others to add their comments?
- ☐ Invite the learners to propose and discuss optional strategies that could be used at those decision points?
- ☐ Invite learners to role play some of the options?
- ☐ Temporarily stop the review process if any learners broke the ground rules?
- ☐ At the end of the review session, give learners a chance to summarize what they learned as well as other issues they want to explore and skills they want to practice?

From: Westberg, J., Jason, H. *Teaching Creatively with Video: Fostering Reflection, Communication and Other Clinical Skills,* New York: Springer Publishing Co., 1994.

Part II

Using Video in Clinical Supervision

Educating learners in clinical settings, such as health care centers, hospitals, and nursing homes, can be challenging. To help learners reflect on and critique their work, to provide them with meaningful feedback, and to evaluate their work, all require that we observe them in action. And we need access to what they are thinking and feeling as they work with patients, families, and others. However, our own responsibilities can make it difficult to observe our learners when, or as much as, we need to. And because many learners (especially beginners) are unconsciously incompetent in many areas, their reports of what they did cannot be depended on as adequate or complete descriptions of what happened.

Video can help us with these challenges. Using video we can observe learners as they care for patients and carry out other tasks, even if we were not present when the event occurred. We can also watch all or parts of the event on a monitor, in a precepting room or other area, providing that our learner and the patient are aware that they are being observed.

In addition, video enables us to facilitate our learners' reflection and self-critique and provide them with feedback from ourselves, their peers, and their patients. After taping our learners, we and they can review the recording one-on-one. And we can invite the patient to join us for some or all of the session. Another option is for us to supervise a small group of learners as they take turns reviewing their tapes with each other. Or if we have prepared them to do so, a small group of learners can take turns reviewing their tapes without us. (We call both of these latter strategies *peer review*.) There is even the option of having the patient join us in the group.

Learners can be videotaped during clinical learning experiences (CLEs) to give them and you information about their strengths and needs that can guide their learning. Review sessions can also give them more general insights about themselves, other people, and the process of health care. And learners' recordings can be used to make judgments about their progress or to determine whether they have accomplished the goals of a CLE. As we explain shortly, we recommend that videotaping *not* be used only for summative evaluations (i.e., grading learners).

In Chapter 5 we focus on preparing for and making recordings of learners and their patients. Chapters 6–9 deal with the process of reviewing video recordings of learners engaged in tasks they are learning to do (e.g., interviewing or counseling patients). In Chapter 6 we highlight the role of the learner in the review process; in Chapter 7 we examine the teacher's role in providing feedback. We have artificially separated these roles for ease of discussion. In practice, the learner's self-critique and the teacher's feedback are not monologues; they are dynamic, intertwined events. When effectively done, the learner's self-critique often leads to the teacher's critique of the learner's self-critique as well as to the teacher's contributions of additional observations and feedback. The teacher's feedback, in turn, can lead to more reflection and self-critique by the learner. When the review includes the patient (Chapter 9), the process becomes a three-way conversation. (For some purposes, we suggest occasionally videotaping learners in clinical settings with simulated patients who then participate in the review session.) When the review includes the learner, the teacher, and the learner's peers (Chapter 8), the process can include dynamic, mutually reinforcing interactions among all members of the group.

CHAPTER 5

Preparing for and Making Recordings

A growing number of health care facilities and hospitals have video cameras installed in exam rooms, counseling rooms, and other areas so that learners can be videotaped while caring for patients/clients. Some institutions have precepting rooms with video playback equipment, where teachers and learners can review videotapes. And some programs have mechanisms for obtaining patients' written consents and for making and reviewing recordings. If you teach in such an institution, you and your learners are fortunate.

More typically, institutions have some equipment and audiovisual staff who can assist you. Some institutions have neither equipment nor staff. Fortunately, a growing number of teachers have access to camcorders (combination cameras and recorders made for the home market). Even if their institutions have professional equipment, some teachers choose to use camcorders because they are less cumbersome than the heavier professional equipment.

Much of this chapter is devoted to the educational and psychological issues involved in preparing yourself, learners, and patients for being videotaped, and to the important details needing your attention, if tapings are to go smoothly and result in successful recordings. We also discuss some of the mechanisms that need to be put into place if you and others want to videotape learners on a regular basis. We have included some technical information for readers who will make their own recordings or who want to be able to supervise others (e.g., audiovisual staff, learners) who will make or help make the recordings.

Our focus is on making recordings that provide the images and other information you and your learners need for reviewing their work. We do not discuss the issues related to making high-quality recordings that are suitable for distribution to others.

If you are going to make your own recordings and are new to doing so, we recommend first recording a learner and a patient who are in a fixed position (e.g., sitting in chairs talking with each other, as in an interview, a patient education session, or a counseling session). As we explain shortly, this can be done with a camera on a fixed tripod. Later you might want to try videotaping learners as they move around doing such things as examining patients, changing bandages, and doing various procedures.

In this chapter, we

- discuss issues and considerations involved in preparing for and making recordings
- provide suggestions for (1) preparing for making recordings, (2) preparing learners for being recorded, and (3) making recordings.

In Chapter 8 we provide suggestions for preparing patients for being recorded.

ISSUES AND CONSIDERATIONS

Some learners may be uneasy about being videotaped.

Learners who have never been videotaped or who have had negative experiences with being taped may initially be uneasy about being taped. Learners who are observed infrequently are also more likely to be uneasy. They may logically worry that they have a lot riding on the one or two videorecording sessions they face. They are also likely to be uncomfortable if videotaping is used only for giving them a grade or for determining whether they have completed a clinical learning experience. As we will discuss more fully, learners are most likely to be comfortable with being videotaped if they are taped regularly throughout their clinical learning and if the focus is consistently on providing them with constructive help.

Some patients may be uneasy about being videotaped.

Patients are likely to be uneasy about being videotaped if they are worried that their privacy will be violated. This will especially be the case if they anticipate needing to talk about sensitive matters or are worried that they will be taped during examinations or procedures involving intimate parts of their body. Once patients are helped to understand that their privacy will be respected and that their willingness to be videotaped will enable a student or resident to have an important learning experience, they are more likely to agree to participate in the process. In Chapter 9 we discuss preparing patients for being videotaped.

Patients must give their informed consent.

Patients should not be videotaped without first giving their written informed consent. This consent needs to indicate how the recording will be used. In some institutions, where a lot of videotaping is done, patients are asked to provide "blanket" (overall) written consents when they first register. Some also get patients' written consents each time they are taped.

When patients first visit a health center, hospital, or other health care facility where teaching is provided, they should certainly be informed about the presence of learners and how they will be affected by this program (e.g., be cared for by students and residents). If videotaping is part of the program, they should also be informed about the purpose of the taping and how it might affect them. (Telling patients about the videotaping is particularly important if television cameras are permanently mounted in exam rooms.) Even if patients sign a blanket consent form when they visit the facility, we recommend that a separate written consent be sought each time they are videotaped. Patients who generally feel comfortable being videotaped may not want to be taped on a particular visit. Also, when you, your learner, or someone else secures patients' consents, you can invite their questions and ensure that they are still comfortable with the process.

Some educators contend that learners should not know when they are being videotaped.

In some institutions that have video cameras installed in exm rooms, learners—and in some cases, patients—report not knowing when they are being videotaped. (Presumably, patients have given a blanket consent.) Some teachers at these institutions don't want learners to know when they are being taped, on the assumption that the learners will not be natural, and will modify what they do in an effort to get a good grade.

Initially, some learners might make an effort to do what they think is expected of them in an attempt to get a positive evaluation, but we find most act quite naturally. Even if they want to act in particular ways, learners are restricted in what they can do. They can only do what is in their repertoire; they cannot use a strategy they feel will please their teacher if they have not yet learned that strategy.

Learners who do not know when they are being observed but know that they *might* be can actually experience an enhanced sense of anxiety that can, if anything, cause a degradation in their performance. We do not see this as a decent trade-off in the quest for spontaneity. Also, since trust is so key to our relationships with learners and to our learners' relationships with their patients, we recommend that learners and patients always be dealt with honestly and openly, and be informed whenever they are being videotaped.

You are most likely to get an accurate impression of learners if you videotape them regularly.

Multiple observations over time provide the most accurate information about learners' capabilities. The more "snapshots" you have of learners, the more likely that your composite picture of them will be accurate and realistic. If, over time, you observe learners in a nonthreatening way and if those learners have come to trust you, they are less likely to be nervous or artificial when you observe them. By videotaping learners regularly, you can monitor their progress, detecting potential problems as soon as possible.

There are several advantages and one potential disadvantage to permanently installing video equipment in clinical settings.

In thinking through the pros and cons, it is important to visualize the setup. Typically, cables from the camera are run through the ceiling to the video recorder and monitor, which are in another room (e.g., a precepting room). Most cameras are turned on or shut off at the video recorder. Unless the camera is mounted out of reach, a lens cap is often placed on the camera when it is not in use so that patients will not be concerned that they are being observed or recorded without their knowledge.

Having cameras installed in the rooms where you want to tape your learners can greatly facilitate your videotaping program by saving you the trouble of arranging for and setting up video equipment every time you want to make a recording. In addition, you probably won't need to be concerned about rearranging the furniture; it is likely to be located optimally for videotaping. That task was probably done when the equipment was installed. Further, a mounted camera is usually less of a presence and less disruptive than a temporary camera on a tripod.

The disadvantage to having a camera permanently mounted on the wall in the room is that the image you capture may not be as adequate as the image(s) you can get from a camera mounted on a movable tripod. This is particularly true if the fixed camera has been mounted so high on the wall that the resulting picture is a "bird's-eye view"—a shot that looks down on the heads of the subjects. Also, if your camera provides only a fixed image (you can't *pan* the camera left or right or *tilt* it up or down) and your subjects are out of the range of the camera or move in or out of the shot, the resulting recording will be suboptimal.

Having a well-located precepting room with video equipment can facilitate the video-assisted review program.

Teachers who have to hunt for a room and for playback equipment each time they want to review tapes with learners are likely to become discouraged and to avoid making and reviewing videotapes. Having a precepting room with recording equipment gives the message that the video program is an integral part of the overall educational program. Locating the precepting room in a convenient place is also important. If you and your learners need to stay in the patient care area but the precepting room is a few minutes walk away, you may not use the room and the equipment very often. If, however, the precepting room is in the clinical area, you will probably use it more frequently, and you can more easily view the recording while it is being made. Also, you can have video support for any immediate feedback and advice you want to give to your preceptee.

Videotaping can disrupt patient care.

Bringing a camera and tripod into a health care center or hospital and videotaping learners and their patients can be disruptive, particularly if the staff is not aware that there will be taping. Shortly, we provide several suggestions regarding what you can do prior to and during the video recording so as to minimize the disruption. One of the keys to minimizing disruption is planning ahead.

The challenges involved in making recordings are linked to the kinds of images you need.

The easiest recording is based on a *static* (fixed) shot of two people (e.g., a learner and a patient) sitting in closely placed chairs and talking with each other. You can put the camera on a tripod, align the picture you want, set the equipment for recording, and leave the room while the taping is done. If your subjects are moving around, the challenge is increased because you or someone else must then operate the camera, following the action and even deciding whether you want to shift between wider shots and close-up images (e.g., of the learner's hands as she does a particular maneuver) or particular points of view. If you have more than two subjects (e.g., your learner is counseling a family of four), your challenge is also increased. A wide shot that includes all of the subjects may not give you the facial detail that is desirable for most review sessions, so you will probably have to move the camera from person to person as they talk or react. Being able to follow the action with smooth, well-paced moves, even with the camera on a tripod, takes practice.

Making smooth moves while hand-holding the camera (not using a tripod) is even more difficult.

The equipment used for making the recording should be compatible with the format of the equipment used for reviewing the tape.

As we discussed in Chapter 1, video equipment and tapes are available in several formats. Most equipment will play only one format, although some equipment can play two related formats.

SUGGESTIONS

PREPARING FOR MAKING RECORDINGS

- **Be clear about the purposes for making the recording.**

As with any educational event, be clear about what you hope your learners will achieve. It might be that you have a direct goal for your learners (e.g , that they will have greater awareness of the nonverbal messages they send to others with whom they are communicating). Or you might want your learners to formulate their own goals.

- **Be clear about the kinds of shots that are needed.**

As we've indicated and will discuss further, the kinds of shots you need can affect who must operate the equipment and what kind of equipment you need. Decide not only who should be in the shots but whether you should follow your subjects with the camera as they move around and whether you need special shots, such as close-ups.

- **Determine what video equipment you need and arrange to get it.**

If you have some choice about the type of equipment you use, the way you will use the tape and the circumstances in which you will be making the recording should help guide your decision. Recordings made on consumer-level equipment (e.g., VHS, 8mm) are perfectly adequate for one-time review sessions with individual students or with small groups. If you need higher-quality recordings, perhaps for editing, duplicating, and distribution, you may be able to use Hi8, S-VHS, or one of the professional formats we described in Chapter 3. Compact equipment (e.g., 8mm) is desirable in many circumstances, especially busy emergency rooms, operating rooms, and hospital floors where you may need to move your equipment quickly and unobtrusively.

Unless you have a *Steadicam jr* (a device enabling the camera to be moved while keeping the picture steady) and someone who is skilled at using it, or a camera with built-in optical compensation for hand-held shaking, most recordings should be done with the camera on a tripod. Most newer equipment does not require auxiliary lighting, unless you need high-quality pictures. Because of the noisiness of many patient care areas, it can be useful to have microphones for your subjects, rather than depending on the camcorder's built-in microphones.

- **Determine who will operate the camera.**

If the camera is permanently mounted in the room where the videotaping will be done and the camera is controlled from a recorder in another room, you or the learner can turn on the recording machine and set the buttons for *record* immediately prior to the event being recorded. (You or the learner may also need to turn the camera on and set it to record.)

If the camera will be mounted on a tripod and then left in a fixed position throughout the recording, you or someone else will need to *frame* the picture (i.e., ensure that the subjects are in the picture and that you are getting the needed details). Then, when your subjects are ready, you can set the equipment for record and leave the room, or the learner could try to frame the picture, start the recording, and then sit down in a chair that was placed to be in the shot. (See Chapter 2 for a discussion of steps people can take in making recordings of themselves and their patients or interviewees.) If, however, there is a chance that the learner might accidentally move the camera as she or he sits down or if having to start the recording might interfere with the learner doing the task being recorded, then it's preferable for you or someone else to frame the picture and start the recording.

If the images that are needed require operating the camera during the recording, you may want to be the videographer. But if you feel your presence could interfere with the event you are taping or if you don't feel you can handle the camera adequately, consider having an audiovisual technician or professional videographer operate the camera.

When selecting someone else to operate the camera, be sure that person understands what shots are needed and how he or she needs to behave in the environment in which the taping is being done. For example, camera operators must be respectful to patients, learners, and staff and make sure that they don't interfere with patient care. If they are taping in an operating room, they need to wear scrubs and stay away from sterile areas.

- **Work out a policy for how the tapes will be used and where and for how long they will be kept.**

Some tapes are used only for review sessions. Others are kept for faculty development or other teaching purposes. Learners might keep their own tapes or you or a staff person might be responsible for them. Tapes can be erased or recorded over immediately after they are reviewed, or they can be kept for a period of time. Decisions regarding how the tapes will be used, who will see them, who might have access to them, where and how they will be stored, and how long they will be kept should all be made prior to making the recordings. Ethical and educational considerations need to be taken into account when making these decisions. For example, it is often desirable for learners to be able to keep their tapes so they can study them multiple times. But if the recordings are of real patients, care needs to be taken to ensure that the tapes are not viewed by persons who are not covered by the patients' informed consents, such as learners' family members or friends.

- **Make sure you have appropriate consent forms.**

Most institutions that have video-recording equipment have patient consent forms. Unfortunately, as we discussed in Chapter 2, many of these forms are written in perplexing legalese. If you need to develop a form or are in a position to revise one, make certain it is written in clear, straightforward language, and be sure that the form indicates how the recordings will be used. Institutions usually have their legal counsel review, if not write, the consent forms.

- **Make sure there is a satisfactory strategy for securing consent from patients.**

If your institution has a policy of verbally informing new patients about the existence of the teaching program, including the videotaping of learners, be sure that the people who explain the program to patients are supportive of it and are able to explain it in a clear, nonthreatening way. (During decades of securing consents for taping from patients, the few refusals we have had were in situations in which the person requesting the consent was ambivalent or negative about the videotaping.) As we've indicated, we strongly recommend informing patients each time they will be videotaped.

Often the faculty member obtains the informed consent. In some institutions, administrative or nursing staff members obtain patients' consents and put the signed consent forms in the patients' charts. In other institutions, learners secure the written consents from their patients. Doing this gives learners an opportunity to explain to their patients how the process will help their education and to express their appreciation.

- **Identify the most suitable room or space for videotaping.**

When looking for a setting for taping, consider the following questions:

- Is there adequate space both for the activity that is to be taped and for the video equipment as well perhaps as a camera operator?
- Is the room quiet enough so that you can get clear audio at the needed level of quality? (Recordings made for editing and distribution need to be at a higher standard than recordings made for internal uses, but clearly intelligible audio is vital for optimal educational impact.)
- Are there any special lighting challenges? If so, can they be managed?
- Will the videotaping interfere with regular clinical activities? If so, can that problem be managed during the time needed for the videotaping?

If the available lighting is low or you are working with an older camera, you may need supplementary lighting. If possible, avoid a room in which you will be forced to *backlight* your subjects (i.e., videotaping them against a bright background, such as an uncovered window or other light source that is brighter than the light falling on the side of the subjects closest to the camera). Excessive backlighting causes the important elements of the picture, such as your subjects' faces, to be in shadows, making it difficult to see their eyes and facial expressions—information that is often needed when reviewing learner-patient interactions. Better cameras have a manual iris or a backlight compensation switch that allows users to minimize the deleterious effects of backlighting.

- **Talk with personnel at the site who might be affected by the videotaping.**

If the taping will take place in a clinical area or another space over which people feel ownership, consider talking in advance with a key person at the site, even if that person does not make the ultimate administrative decision about whether you are permitted to use the space. People who work at the site can give you important information; and if they know what you need and want, they are likely to help create a better atmosphere than might be the case if they feel that the taping is intruding on them or their space.

- **Arrange for use of the site.**

Although making sure to schedule the use of the site for a particular date and time may seem like an obvious step to take, not everyone remembers to make such arrangements. If all of the other details have been taken care of but the room turns out not to be available when needed, the costs, delays, embarrassments, and aggravations can be considerable.

- **Select the patient(s)/client(s) who will be videotaped.**

In Chapter 4 we discuss issues to consider when selecting simulated patients/clients. In Chapter 9 we discuss issues to consider when selecting real patients/clients. If students or residents are going to be videotaped with their patients or clients, they can be involved in selecting them and securing their consent.

PREPARING LEARNERS

If you have already videotaped the learners in a classroom or conference setting, you will not need to take some of the following steps.

- **Be sure that the learners understand how and when they will be taped and how and when they will review the tape.**

Your learners' level of anxiety is likely to be lower if they know what will be happening.

- **Be sure learners are clear about their goals and what they are expected to do during the videotaping.**

Most times the learners' goal during the taping is to do the task at hand as well as they can, whereas the goal during the review session might be to reflect on their thought processes during the encounters. On other occasions learners might be using the taped encounters in part to practice or refine new skills. For example, a learner might be trying to be less judgmental during interactions with patients. Check with your learners to be sure they know what is expected of them while they are being taped.

- **Be sure that the learners understand what will happen to the tape after the review session.**

Your learners' trust in you and the process is likely to be facilitated if they know their privacy will be respected and that their recordings will be used to help, not hurt, them.

- **Assess your learners' prior experiences with being videotaped and seeing themselves on television.**

See Chapter 4.

- **Assess your learners' prior experiences and levels of comfort with using video for reviewing the practice of new skills.**

See Chapter 4.

- **Consider first videotaping learners in simulated circumstances.**

Being videotaped in a real clinical setting can be discomforting for some learners, even for some graduate students and residents. To reduce this anxiety and to help prepare learners for the experience of being taped with real patients in a clinical setting, consider first videotaping them in a safe, nonthreatening, simulated environment, with a peer or a simulated patient/client. (See Chapter 4.) Also consider taping them with a simulated patient/client in a real health care setting.

- **Consider giving learners responsibility for some of the process of making the recording.**

Again in the spirit of helping learners become partners in their learning, think through ways they can assist with recording themselves or a peer. They might take responsibility for making the arrangements for getting the equipment and even help to set it up. If they are working in a facility with permanently mounted cameras, they might both arrange to see patients in a room with a camera and to have the camera switched on for a particular encounter.

- **Consider inviting your learners to identify the encounters they want to tape.**

Our hope is that learners will find that reviewing recordings of their work is so valuable that they will take the initiative in asking to be taped again. For example, in some programs, learners who anticipate having difficulty working with a particular patient ask to be taped with that patient so that they can review what occurs and learn from it. To move learners toward becoming more active in their education, you can ask them to identify encounters with which they anticipate wanting help.

MAKING RECORDINGS

The following suggestions deal with making straightforward, simple recordings, particularly recordings of learners with patients. We don't provide details about technical issues. There are many books and magazines on that subject (see "Further Readings on Video Production" at the end of this chapter). As an early step, if time has elapsed since you spoke with the learner or patient about the videotaping, review the process with them.

- **Decide where the subjects will sit or stand.**

Particularly when you are videotaping in a small area, such as an exam room, carefully think through where to position your subjects. Some factors to consider:

- Don't position your subjects in front of a strong light source, such as a window, because you could have problems with backlighting (see above).
- If you are trying to get two people into the picture (a 2-shot) in a small room, you may need to figure out a way to get the camera as far away from your subjects as possible. A good *wide angle lens* or a *zoom lens* adjusted to its wide-angle setting is usually needed. Some rooms are so small that you need to place the camera in the hall to achieve the distance needed between the camera and the subjects. (This strategy cannot be used if there is noise or traffic in the hall.)
- If you are trying to get a 2-shot in a small room, your subjects may have to sit closer to each other than they normally would.
- If you will be making many similar recordings in a particular room, make note of how you position your subjects so that you won't have to rethink the positioning each time you make a recording.
- If the subjects have to change their positions (e.g., from chairs to an exam table) and are in a small room, you will probably have to stop the action and reposition the camera (and lights, if used) before continuing to record.

- **Assure that you have adequate lighting but avoid backlighting.**

The general overhead lighting in most exam rooms is usually sufficient. Some older cameras, as we've mentioned, need supplemental lighting even in moderately lighted rooms.

- **Make sure that the audio is adequate for your purposes.**

Before starting the full recording, record your subjects for 10 or 20 seconds as they talk in normal voices. Then play back the tape and check if the audio is adequate for your purposes. If you can't hear your subjects clearly, consider putting an external microphone between them rather than relying on the camera's built-in microphone. Or put a lavaliere microphone on each subject, in which case you will need an *audio mixer* (an electronic device that enables the mixing of two or more independent audio sources that might each require separate levels of amplification). Also, control for extraneous sound as much as possible. For example, temporarily turn off the air handler and shut the door if necessary.

Suggestions for Using a Fixed Camera Without a Camera Operator

- **Be sure you are getting the shot you want.**

When using a fixed camera without a camera operator, you have only one shot or point of view; that is, only one way in which the entire recording is framed. First, you must ensure that you will be getting a usable shot. The camera's framing must be checked before each recording to be sure that it has not been moved and that it is still framing the area where your subjects will be sitting. Second, your shot should be linked to the purpose of the recording. If, for example, the learner will be using the recording to study the patient and the patient is sitting to the right of the learner, the camera can be pointed to slightly left of center in a 2-shot. Or you can shift the placement of your subjects so that you are shooting the patient from over the learner's shoulder. (See Figures 2.2–2.4.)

If you are recording an interview, try having the camera lens at about your subjects' eye levels so that you have optimal access to their facial expressions. Many cameras that are attached to the ceilings or walls of exam rooms are placed too high, producing the "bird's-eye views" we've discussed. If such is the case at your location, try to arrange for the cameras to be lowered.

If you are shooting an interview or conversation, regardless of which camera placement you use, make your shots as *tight* as possible—eliminate extra space around your subjects so that you are close enough to get the best possible views of their facial expressions. (Don't make the shot so tight that your subjects might easily move out of the frame.) If you are shooting a procedure or an exam, you will probably need a *looser* shot most of the time to allow for movement and to encompass all of the unpredictable action.

- **Ask your subjects to limit their movements.**

Frame the picture to allow for your subjects' normal movements (e.g., some minor shifting in their seats). Then, before starting the recording, have your subjects talk and move normally for a short while so you can let them know if they go out of frame. If necessary, ask them to avoid excessive movement or shifting in their chairs, although doing so carries the risk of making them self-conscious and causing them to behave in ways that are not fully natural. To help reduce the risk of distracting movements, avoid using chairs that can tilt or swivel.

- **Protect the camera from children and vice versa.**

If the camera is not well secured or well out of their way, children's curiosity can cause them to hurt themselves or damage the equipment. Or they might be so curious that they will spend most of the session standing in front of the camera, leaving you with numerous out-of-focus close-ups of them, instead of the images you need.

Suggestions for Operating the Camera

- **Change shots as slowly and smoothly as possible.**

As we discussed in Chapter 4, jerky or excessive movements (including too many *pans* and *zooms*) can be disruptive to viewers. If your subjects are moving, you need to follow their action, but try to do so as smoothly as possible.

- **Use a tripod as much as possible.**

Tripods enable you to keep your shots smooth and steady, which is desirable.

- **If the camera or subjects need to move, double-check the focus.**

Most contemporary camcorders have automatic focusing. Some can be switched to manual focusing. Some autofocus systems are fooled by reflective objects or uneven lighting, so if you are relying on a camcorder's automatic capability, double check that no problems are being introduced. If the camera or subjects move, the focusing must be rechecked each time, especially if the camera is set for manual focusing.

- **If you want learners to analyze the recording, avoid directing their attention with in-camera editing.**

Whenever we change the framing of a shot, we cause viewers to shift their attention. Such in-camera editing is important for some uses (especially demonstrations and explicit instruction), but is not appropriate for tapes that are meant to provide opportunities for reviews of clinical or other performance. For more on this subject, see Chapter 4.

General Suggestions

- **Test the equipment before making the recording.**

See Chapter 4.

- **Have a mechanism that lets subjects know when they are being recorded.**

If you are using video equipment that is permanently installed in an exam room, it might not be clear when it is in use, unless a light on the camera comes on whenever the camera is recording. As a courtesy, even as a legal precaution, work out some system so that people always know when they are being viewed or recorded.

- **Have a mechanism that allows subjects to stop the recording, if appropriate.**

Occasionally, a patient or learner might want to stop a recording. For example, during an interview, a patient who had agreed to be interviewed but not examined on camera might want to show the learner a rash on her breast. If a camera operator is in the room, the patient can simply ask for time out, and the camera operator can turn the camera off and temporarily leave the room. If the camera is on a tripod in the room and there is no camera operator, the learner can temporarily stop the recording. If the camera is permanently installed in the room and not being monitored once it begins recording, learners can be provided with a lens cap that they can temporarily place over the lens. Some sites have installed blinds that can be pulled to cut off the view of installed cameras. If you or someone else is operating the camera, the learner or patient can ask you to stop the recording.

- **Make sure that patients and others are thanked for their help.**

Sometimes learners take the help they receive from patients and others for granted. If you are concerned that such might be the case with some learners, try ensuring that they understand and express their indebtedness to others, especially patients and staff.

FURTHER READINGS ON VIDEO PRODUCTION

Books

Lewis, R. (1987). *The home video maker's handbook.* New York: Crown.

Millerson, G. (1985). *The technique of television production* (11th ed.). London and Boston: Focal Press.

Morley, J. (1992). *Script writing for high impact video: Imaginative approaches for delivering factual information.* Belmont, CA: Wadsworth Publishing Company.

Shook, F. (1989). *Television field production and reporting.* New York and London: Longman.

Wurtzel, A. (1983). *Television production.* New York: McGraw-Hill.

Zettl, H. (1984). *Television production handbook* (4th ed.). Belmont, CA: Wadsworth Publishing Company.

Journals/Magazines

Of interest to educational/industrial video producers:

A / V Video, Montage Publishing, Inc.; Knowledge Industry Publications, Inc.; 701 Westchester Avenue, White Plains, NY 10604 (free to educators).

Intended for consumer-level users:

Videomaker, PO Box 469026, Escondido, CA 92046-9838.

Video, 460 West 34th Street, New York, NY 10117-0460.

Appendix 5.1

Self-Checklist: Preparing for Making Recordings

Have I (we) . . .

- ☐ Made certain that I (and my learners) are clear about the purposes of making the recording?
- ☐ Made certain there is clarity about the shots that are needed?
- ☐ Determined what video equipment is needed and made arrangements to get it?
- ☐ Determined who will operate the camera?
- ☐ Worked out a policy for how the tapes will be used and where and for how long they will be kept?
- ☐ Made certain we have appropriate consent forms?
- ☐ Made certain there is a satisfactory strategy for securing consent from patients?
- ☐ Identified a suitable room or space for videotaping?
- ☐ Talked with personnel at the site who might be affected by the videotaping?
- ☐ Arranged for use of the site?
- ☐ Prepared my learners for being videotaped?
- ☐ Made sure that the learners understand how and when they will be taped and how and when we will review the tapes?
- ☐ Made sure learners are clear about their goals and what they are expected to do during the videotaping?
- ☐ Assessed the learners' prior experiences with being videotaped and seeing themselves on television?
- ☐ Assessed the learners' prior experiences and levels of comfort with using video for reviewing the practice of new skills?
- ☐ First videotaped the learners in simulated circumstances?
- ☐ Given learners responsibility for some of the process of making the recordings?
- ☐ Invited the learners to identify the encounters they wanted to tape?
- ☐ Prepared patients for being videotaped? (See Chapter 9.)

From: Westberg, J., Jason, H. *Teaching Creatively with Video: Fostering Reflection, Communication and Other Clinical Skills,* New York: Springer Publishing Co., 1994.

Appendix 5.2

Self-Checklist: Making Recordings

Did I . . .

- ☐ (If time had elapsed since I spoke with them about the videotaping.) Review the process.
- ☐ Decide where the subjects would sit or stand?
- ☐ Ensure that there was adequate lighting, and avoid backlighting?
- ☐ Ensure that the audio was adequate for our purposes?

If we used a fixed camera without an operator:

- ☐ Make sure we got the shot we needed?
- ☐ Ask the subjects to limit their movements?
- ☐ Make sure the equipment was protected from children and vice versa?

If I operated the camera (or had someone else operate it):

- ☐ Change shots as slowly and smoothly as possible?
- ☐ Use a tripod, even if I had to move the tripod to follow the action (unless I had and could use a Steadicam jr for situations in which much movement was needed)?
- ☐ Double-check the focus, especially if the camera or subjects needed to move?
- ☐ Avoid directing the viewers' attention with in-camera editing?

Whether the camera was fixed or operated by me or someone else:

- ☐ Test the equipment before making the recording?
- ☐ Have a mechanism that let subjects know when they were being recorded?
- ☐ Have a mechanism that allowed subjects to stop the recording if appropriate?
- ☐ Make sure that patients and others were thanked for their help?

From: Westberg, J., Jason, H. *Teaching Creatively with Video: Fostering Reflection, Communication and Other Clinical Skills,* New York: Springer Publishing Co., 1994.

CHAPTER 6

Helping Learners Use Video for Reflection and Self-Assessment

To get maximum value from their formal education and to continue growing after they graduate, students need to be active learners who feel responsible for their own education. Being reflective and self-critical about their learning experiences, both while these experiences are occurring and after they are over, is key to being effective current and continuing learners. Such reflections can result in new questions and insights about learning and about the process of health care. And as learners reflect on their performance, they are developing and reinforcing the important habit of identifying their strengths and the areas needing further work.

Assuring that learners value and regularly engage in reflection and develop the skills needed for constructive self-assessment is a central instructional obligation. As we discuss shortly, video is a powerful tool for helping us with this task.

Learners can review recordings of their work by themselves, with a preceptor during one-on-one supervisory sessions, with a teacher and a group of peers (see Chapter 8), or with just a group of their peers. When a patient is present during the review session, learners can focus their reflections on their interactions with the patient (see Chapter 9).

During one-on-one supervisory sessions, our tasks include facilitating the learners' reflections and self-assessments as well as providing our own observations, insights, and suggestions. In general, beginning by inviting our learners' reflections and self-assessments while withholding our feedback is beneficial both for us and our learners.

Effective supervisory sessions are dynamic dialogues between teacher and learner. Because of the complexity of this dialogue, we focus in this chapter on facilitating the learner's involvement in the dialogue. In the next chapter, we examine our role as providers of feedback in this dialogue.

In this chapter, we

- examine the rationale for (1) inviting learners to critique their work before we provide our feedback, and (2) inviting learners to use video to help them reflect on and digest their experiences and progress
- identify and discuss issues and concerns to have in mind when inviting learners to assess their own performance
- provide practical suggestions for (1) preparing learners for reviewing recordings of their clinical performance and (2) reviewing recordings of the learners' clinical performance.

REASONS FOR INVITING LEARNERS' SELF-CRITIQUE BEFORE PROVIDING OUR FEEDBACK

Routinely inviting learners' reflections and self-assessments can help them develop the lifelong habit of taking charge of their education.

Inviting learners to reflect on their work before providing your observations and critique sends the message that you want the review process to be a mutual effort and that their contributions are vital. You can open review sessions with this invitation and repeat the invitation multiple times during a session. If you use this approach routinely during supervisory sessions, in time learners likely begin offering their self-critiques automatically, without waiting for you to ask for it. After providing their self-critique, if you have earned their trust, they may even invite your critique of their critique and ask for other feedback. Most important, they will be on their way to adopting the vital career habit of taking responsibility for their learning.

You can check your hypotheses about your learners' performance, reducing the likelihood that you'll give inappropriate feedback.

Our observations of learners will often cause us to generate hypotheses about their intentions and capabilities. If we provide feedback to our learners on the basis of our hypotheses, without first indirectly or directly checking those hypotheses with them, we risk giving inappropriate feedback to our learners and even losing some credibility with them. Let's say a teacher and a student are reviewing a video recording of a patient interaction that the learner recently completed but the teacher didn't observe. The patient seems eager to talk about the conflict she is having with her boss, but the student interrupts the patient, shifting the discussion back to the particulars about the patient's headaches. If the teacher asks the student to stop the tape and voices his assumption that the student is being insensitive to the patient's eagerness to talk about her boss, he may or may not be correct. If, instead, he first invites the student to reflect aloud on what he was thinking and doing, he may learn that during a previous interview, which the teacher hadn't seen, the student explored the patient's relationship with her boss in depth. Now, the student reports he feels he needs to explore some other issues.

When we invite our learners' comments before offering feedback and also, if necessary, follow up on their comments with questions, we are gathering valuable diagnostic information that can help us to confirm or reject our hypotheses about their performance and capabilities. With this information, we are likely to be more on target with our feedback.

If we rush to provide our feedback, we can lose access to valuable information from our learners.

Even if our feedback is accurate, giving this feedback to learners prematurely blocks the opportunity to discover what they would say about their performance if they weren't influenced by our comments. Once they've heard our comments, there is a risk that learners (particularly those who are trying to please us) may try to give us the information they think we want to hear and withhold information that they think we don't want to hear or information they think might work against them—including information about their worries or difficulties, which we need if we are to be fully helpful to them.

In addition, when we preempt learners with our observations, we are unlikely to ever know whether they had certain insights or made certain discoveries by themselves. If, for example, we tell a learner that she isn't making adequate eye contact with her client, we may lose the opportunity to know whether she had realized that herself.

When we begin review sessions or key parts of reviews with an invitation to learners to be reflective, the issues they select for review can give us clues about their interests and knowledge. When they appear not to notice important events, we might have a clue that they are unaware of the significance of these events or that the events may cause them discomfort. The accuracy of their critiques and the extent to which they are balanced in their assessments of themselves can give us information about their self-image, their expectations for themselves, and their skills in critiquing the particular capabilities they are reflecting on. Giving premature feedback to learners can rob us of the opportunity to gather this information, which can eliminate our ability to facilitate their learning by providing meaningful feedback.

Even positive feedback, if premature, can squelch some learners.

Even positive feedback can diminish some of the potential value of a learning event, if offered prematurely. If you begin a critique session by telling a student that he did a marvelous job, you may cause him to withhold his concerns that some of what he was thinking or feeling during the taped interaction was inappropriate. Fearing that introducing negative self-critique may diminish your good image of him, he might conceal his observations, and a potentially valuable instructional opportunity would be lost.

The caution about avoiding premature feedback applies particularly to learners you do not yet know well.

Postponing your views is less important if you know learners well and feel they are sufficiently trusting of you that they are not likely to feel stifled by your opinions and feedback.

Learners can feel a greater sense of self-respect and accomplishment if they, rather than we, identify their deficiencies and strengths.

Most of us have trouble receiving negative feedback from others, including our teachers. When you initially withhold your feedback and first invite learners to assess their performance, they can be the ones who identify their deficiencies. If you have succeeded in establishing a trust-based collaborative relationship with them, they will frequently point out the very problems you had intended to identify. You are then in the happy position of being able to give them positive feedback on the perceptiveness of their self-assessment. In fact, some learners are overly negative about their performance.

Learners are likely to feel more ownership of insights that emerge from their discoveries.

Observing learners as they work their way through to new insights and make fresh discoveries about themselves and the world around them can be exhilarating. Also, when learners make discoveries for themselves—even disappointing, negative ones—they are likely to acknowledge and own these insights far more fully than is possible if they hear these insights from others. If we rush to provide our observations and don't give learners a chance to make their own discoveries, we may deprive them of the sense of dignity and deep satisfaction that can accompany self-discovery. And they may not feel ownership of, and may not retain, the insights that we have offered.

REASONS FOR LEARNERS TO USE VIDEO TO "PROCESS" THEIR EXPERIENCES AND PROGRESS

In Chapter 4 we presented some arguments for using video to help learners process their experiences:

- Video playbacks of their performance can provide learners with potent feedback about their efforts.
- Learners can reflect on optional strategies available at decision points.

The following are some additional arguments.

Learners can see themselves as patients/clients see them.

In the words of poet Robert Burns, "O wad some power the Giftie gie us / To see oursels as ithers see us." Meaningful learning and growth require the power that Burns appealed for. Technology has given us that power. Many of us are surprised when we first hear the sound of our recorded voice. Some of us are shocked when we first see ourselves on video. With video, our learners have the unique opportunity to see and hear themselves as their patients see and hear them. And they can compare how they imagined they appeared to their patients with the more objective view they get from watching themselves on video. Typically, they are challenged to readjust their self-image. Many find it a humbling experience and may first dwell unduly on subtle mannerisms and characteristics that they regard negatively, although others seldom notice these details. When working with learners who are new to being videotaped, you may want to provide time and support during this adjustment phase.

Video playbacks of their work allow learners (and teachers) to see things they missed during live interactions.

While observing learners who are engaged in clinical activities, we can't take in everything that is happening. Similarly, while caring for patients, learners can't focus on everything that they and their patients say and do. Reviewing videotapes of their interactions with patients enables them (and us) to pick up details missed during the live interactions and to consider more deeply those events and reflections that may have been glossed over under the pressure of the original encounter.

Video playbacks prompt learners to recall what they were thinking and feeling during clinical events.

Immediately following a patient encounter, learners can usually recall some of what they were thinking and feeling during that encounter. Yet, typically, they have already lost access to some of the details of their thinking, even the progression of their ideas.

And they have lost some of the vividness of their feelings. As time passes, they forget more and more of what occurred, making it difficult, even impossible, to pursue a fully meaningful review of their experiences in that encounter.

When learners' reviews are supported by video recordings, they see images and hear words and sounds that can help them recapture what they were thinking and feeling during various stages of the original event, especially if the review is done quite soon after the event. If they are willing to share their internal experiences with you, you can help them gain valuable insights about their functioning in such situations.

In the early 1960s, while at Michigan State University, Kagan (1978, 1984a, 1984b) developed a method for teaching interpersonal skills to psychiatrists, counselors, other mental health workers, and educators which involved the review of videotapes of their interactions with patients/clients (see also Spivack & Kagan, 1972). In the mid-1960s, this method—interpersonal process recall (IPR)—was modified for use with medical students (Jason, Kagan, Werner, Elstein, & Thomas, 1971). Students were videotaped while interviewing an actor who had been prepared to play the role of a patient. Three or 4 of the student's classmates, a physician-preceptor, and a mental health professional (typically a psychiatrist or psychologist) all witnessed the original interview and were present, along with the student and "patient," during the recall session. Students were told to stop the videotape whenever the playback helped them remember any thoughts, feelings, goals, impressions, or images they had during the session, as well as anything they had been tempted to say or do. Students were asked to try to recall how they wanted to be perceived by the patient, how they thought the patient perceived their behavior, and how satisfied they were with their own behavior during the interview. Students also received feedback from the simulated patient and preceptors.

IPR, or modified versions of IPR, has been used over the years in many medical schools (Kahn, Cohen, & Jason, 1979b), residency programs (Kahn, Cohen, & Jason, 1979a), nursing schools (Sparks, Vitalo, Cohen, & Kahn, 1980) and in other health professions training programs (Westberg, Kahn, Cohen, & Friel, 1980). Researchers have found statistically significant gains in learners who have participated in courses that used the IPR model (Feidel &

Bolm, 1981; Novik, 1978; Resnikoff, 1968; Robbins et al., 1974). For a description of the process, see Kagan and Kagan (1991).

Learners can focus on the patient.

When caring for patients, beginners can get so distracted by such tasks as examining the patient and writing in the chart that they have minimal residual capacity for observing and listening to the patient. Video enables learners to review recordings of their interactions with patients while focusing exclusively on the patient. If they are confused about a patient's question or response, they can replay that segment multiple times, trying to understand what was going on. (In Chapter 9 we discuss ways to elicit patients' reflections on what they were thinking and feeling.)

Video recordings capture nonverbal communication for analysis and discussion.

Nonverbal communication is an important part of health care. Health professionals who are aware of and understand the possible meanings of their nonverbal communications as well as the nonverbal communications of their patients can use this information to provide sensitive and responsive health care.

Many beginners find it difficult to focus on the nonverbal component of the communications in which they are involved, in addition to all of their other tasks. And, of course, none of us can sense all of our own nonverbal communications, or see the communications from patients or others that occur while we are not looking at them. Even when maintaining eye contact with patients, we cannot see gestures and movements that are outside our field of vision (e.g., foot movements), and we can't give patients' behaviors our full attention while reflecting on what they are saying or on what we will say next. Video makes it possible to study and reflect on nonverbal communication in ways that are not otherwise possible.

Video enables learners to see what they have done so that they can make deliberate choices about how to function.

Learners who are not clear about what they are doing when engaged in various clinical tasks cannot make conscious, deliberate choices about their ways of functioning. Learners who become aware of what they are doing—throughout an interaction as well as at key decision points—may be satisfied and decide to continue functioning in the same way. On the other hand, if learners are not satisfied with what they are doing or want to experiment with optional strategies, they can consciously choose to change their behavior.

Video recordings of learners eliminate guesswork and correct errors of recall about the taped events.

When we and a learner review the learner's performance without benefit of video, our supervisory exchange is typically based on our separate memories of what happened. Notes that we made while observing our learner's work can help, but usually we and the student are inescapably left with holes in our memories about exactly what happened. Sometimes we and our learners can be in sharp disagreement.

Video recordings of learners' interviews can eliminate many of these distracting problems. You and your students or residents do not have to guess; you can consult the tape and determine what actually occurred.

Practicing the skills of reviewing experiences after they occur can help students learn to reflect on experiences while they are occurring.

All complex skills, including the capacity to reflect on experiences while they are occurring, need to be practiced. Being reflective during an experience requires the capacity to be in an event while simultaneously reflecting on that event. Often, as we discussed in Chapter 4, it is helpful to practice complex skills in relatively safe, controlled environments before practicing them in the real world in real time. Video-linked review sessions can serve as safe environments for learners to practice their reflective skills.

During some review sessions, learners can focus solely on their reflections and self-assessments. When doing a review, in contrast to functioning in a real environment, they do not need to be simultaneously doing two large tasks: managing their own behavior while also interpreting and responding to their patient's needs. When they are ready, learners can practice being reflective during real patient interactions, perhaps initially focusing on only one issue at a time. While talking with a patient, learners who are able to be reflective can observe the process as it occurs, including their own actions. If they have insight into the process, they can recognize when they are at a decision point and choose the strategy or direction they think will be most fruitful. If the interaction is not going well, they can reflect on what is happening, its possible causes, and some alternative approaches, and perhaps choose to alter what they are saying or doing.

Being reflective during an experience also enables learners to pay attention to issues they want to work on (e.g., how they ask questions, how they use their bodies) and make mental notes regarding events and actions they want to reflect on in greater depth at a later time. As we argue shortly, video enables learners to attend to important issues during the review process, even if they were not aware of these issues during the experience that was video recorded. Most of the time, however, learners' interactions with patients are not videotaped, so if they want to work on particular issues, they need to learn to attend to those issues during the experience itself. (Some learners who have had experience with video-stimulated reflection find themselves able to generate their own "instant replays" in their heads during actual events.)

Note: Some readers might find it helpful to study Schön's work on the reflective practitioners (1983, 1987, 1991).

ISSUES AND CONSIDERATIONS

Video recordings of learners' work typically contain more material than can be reviewed in a single supervisory session.

Recordings of learners doing interviews or other clinical tasks are often 20 minutes or more in length. When guided by a skilled teacher, learners can take an average of at least 5 minutes for reflection and analysis for each minute of recording. In addition, because there are often multiple themes that can be addressed in each learner-patient interaction (e.g., the steps in the learner's thinking, the way the learner prepared the patient for an examination), a single recording can be replayed many times, each time with a different focus. Yet most of us seldom have more than 50 minutes for individual supervisory sessions, so clearly we can't address all of the issues embedded in one video recording and have to set priorities.

Explicit goals can help guide the learner's critique.

In some situations, faculty members have specific capabilities they want learners to work on and demonstrate during the event being taped. For example, a teacher might want learners to demonstrate their capacity to do a complete examination of the heart. In other situations, learners might be invited to propose their own goals. All of us tend to work hardest at achieving those goals we value most, so when setting goals for our learners, it is important to be sure that they understand, accept, and value what we've proposed.

If we and our learners have agreed upon goals for the event being taped and for the review session, these goals can help us set priorities and make the best use of our time together. If, for example, a learner wants to enhance his ability to close interviews effectively, you and he might agree to focus primarily on the last 5 minutes of several interviews.

Learners need goals and standards against which to assess their work.

Self-assessment conducted in a vacuum is unlikely to be effective. Learners need goals and standards against which to measure their performance. In formal educational programs, learners can benefit from the guidance of goals and standards established by their institutions as well as from their own learning goals. Particularly after they graduate, but even during their formal education, health professionals need to be constantly refining their goals, developing new ones and setting new and higher standards, based on the changing world of health care and their rising aspirations for themselves.

Learners need a language and strategies for their self-critique.

Students who have attended traditional educational programs might associate self-critique with the evaluation systems they have experienced, in which judgments made about students' work are reduced to arbitrary, minimally communicative symbols (e.g., excellent, fair, or 98, 74, or A, B, F). If the purpose of the review session you are conducting is to help learners explore and enhance their capacities and to examine their options, you might need to orient them to this approach, even give them questions to guide their critique. In a word, you might need to help them understand that effective evaluation provides explicit guidance, not merely summary judgments.

Learners are often more critical of themselves than we are of them.

Some teachers resist having learners assess their own performance out of concern that learners will be too easy on themselves. Some learners do fail to recognize their shortcomings, but it is important to identify these learners so that corrective guidance can be provided as soon as possible. Actually, many learners are more critical of their performance than are their teachers (Arnold, Willoughby, & Calkins, 1985; Linn, Arostegni, & Zeppa, 1975; Morton & Macbeth, 1977; Stuart, Goldstein, & Snope, 1980).

Until we have succeeded in helping learners be accurate self-evaluators, we have not completed our job of preparing them as independent professionals. We are most likely to learn that they are not yet accurate self-evaluators by inviting the learners' self-assessments. Then we can take whatever steps are indicated to help them work at becoming more accurate.

Typically, learners most need our guidance in critiquing their performance when they are in the early stages of learning new skills.

Studies of athletes have found that those who are in the early stages of learning a skill cannot improve their performance by observing videotapes without the assistance of a coach who draws their attention to the key elements of performance competency (Franks & Maile, 1991). This is likely to be true also for beginning learners in the health professions, who don't yet understand the details and subtleties of the skills they are developing; that is, while they are still unconsciously incompetent. Learners can't make judgments about their competence if they don't yet know what constitutes competence.

Learners need to understand that we don't expect their work to be perfect.

Many learners, particularly those in highly competitive educational programs, are afraid to make mistakes for fear that these mistakes will be held against them. In such circumstances, many learners are especially uneasy about making mistakes that will be preserved on videotape. Apprehensive learners need to be helped to understand that they are in an educational program precisely because they have chosen to develop new skills. In addition, they may need to be helped to understand that when they are learning complex skills we actually expect that they will stumble, go through awkward periods, and make mistakes along the road toward competence.

An open-ended, nonjudgmental approach can facilitate learners' reflection and self-critique.

When interviewing patients, open-ended questions and statements, such as "How can I help you today?" and "Please tell me about your problem" invite patients to tell their stories in their own words. Closed questions, such as "How many times do you get up to urinate during the night?" early in an interview can prematurely reduce the focus of the visit, making it difficult for patients to introduce sensitive, perhaps major, issues that they are uncomfortable presenting at the opening of an encounter.

Beginning patient encounters with a neutral, nonjudgmental approach encourages patients to be candid and to fully disclose their concerns. Conversely, if patients perceive that we have made judgments about them and their situation (particularly negative judgments), they may withhold important information from us. And if we prematurely make judgments about patients and their problems, we risk cutting off our capacity to perceive and use contradictory information that may arise later in the encounter.

For similar reasons, an open-ended, nonjudgmental approach is helpful in facilitating learners' self-critiques. When we open a review session in a nonjudgmental manner with an open-ended statement or question (e.g., "Describe how it went."), we invite learners to share their thoughts in their own words, uninfluenced by us. By having them begin by describing what they did, we are letting them open the self-assessment process with the most "objective" and least potentially discomforting task. Subsequently, with additional questions if needed, we can gradually move them into more challenging tasks, such as reflecting aloud about their feelings and their effectiveness in the encounter.

One of the possible spin-offs of using an open-ended, nonjudgmental approach in review sessions is that learners might be more inclined to use such an open-ended, nonjudgmental approach with their patients and in their teaching. As we discuss elsewhere (Westberg & Jason, 1993), the way we treat learners can have a strong impact on the way that they in turn treat others.

SUGGESTIONS

PREPARING LEARNERS FOR REVIEWING RECORDINGS

When preparing learners for reviewing recordings of their clinical performance, you can work with one student or with a group of students. Most of the following suggestions pertain to both situations. As always, these are suggestions to consider, not rules.

- **If possible, make the review of learners' videotapes a regular part of the educational program.**

The best way to be sure that learners benefit from the power of using video for reflection and self-critique is by making the videotaping of learners a routine part of the educational program—a part of the scenery, if you will. This typically involves having regular schedules for videotaping learners and for supervisory review sessions. The more routine the process, the more quickly will the learners' discomfort diminish and the substantial potential of the strategy be realized.

- **Consider modeling what you want your learners to do: critique a video recording of your work in their presence.**

Perhaps the best way to appreciate the experience of being videotaped and the power of video recordings for reflection and self-assessment is experiencing the process yourself. If you have never seen a recording of yourself at work, be prepared for the possibility of observing behaviors you feel good about as well as behaviors you may want to change. Consider reviewing your initial tapes alone and then with a trusted colleague.

After getting comfortable with the process, consider doing a critique of a portion of one of your video recordings in the presence of learners. You will be providing them with a powerful role-modeling event. You will not only demonstrate *what* to do, but you will convey your *valuing* of self-critique and of video recording as a tool in support of self-critique (if that's how you feel). In addition, by doing your own critique in your learners' presence, you can demystify and detoxify the process for those who are new to, and possibly anxious about, this learning strategy. Your willingness to be openly self-critical about your work conveys a generous gift to your learners that might contribute more to their continuing growth as professionals than almost anything else you can do.

- **Ensure that learners are clear about their learning goals.**

As we indicated above, if you have specific capabilities you want learners to work at and demonstrate, be sure that your intentions are understood and valued by the learners. For example, if you want them to incorporate questions about patients' life-styles into their interviews, be sure that the students understand what information they need to collect and why. If you invite students to propose their own learning goals, help confirm that their goals are worthy and realistic.

Learners may have two sets of goals: their goals for the event being taped (e.g., a patient interview or exam) and their goals for their review session. A student's goals for the event being taped might include one or more of the following, among others:

- using an open-ended approach when initially gathering information
- listening actively to the patient
- presenting information in clear, nontechnical language
- enabling the patient to be an active participant in his care
- being aware of how the patient made her feel
- approaching the patient's problem in a systematic way
- doing a procedure or exam competently and sensitively.

A student's goals for the review session could include
- identifying branch points in the interview
- identifying other strategies that she could have used at the branch points
- trying to recall the thoughts and feelings she experienced but didn't express during the encounter.

- **If learners will be using evaluation forms, be sure they understand each item and how they are to use the form.**

To keep evaluation forms brief, complex concepts are typically presented in an abbreviated form. See Appendix 6.2 for an example of the type of form learners can use.

Review with learners each item on any evaluation forms you want them to use to be sure they understand all aspects. Also, review the key and any other potentially confusing components of the form.

- **Consider first videotaping learners in simulated circumstances.**

Being videotaped for the first time with a patient in a clinical setting can be discomforting for some learners, even for some graduate students and residents. To reduce their anxiety and to help prepare learners for this experience, consider first videotaping them in a classroom with a peer or other person in the role of patient (see Chapter 4). Or tape them with a simulated patient in a real clinical setting.

REVIEWING LEARNERS' RECORDINGS

The following suggestions pertain chiefly to reviewing a video recording with one learner. In Chapter 7 we look at strategies for reviewing recordings with a group of learners. In Chapter 8 we suggest strategies for reviewing recordings with learners and patients.

- **Review the recording as soon after the taped event as possible.**

In our own experience and the experience of others (e.g., Fuller & Manning, 1973), when the review of a learner's video recording is delayed, the recording is less effective in stimulating insight and detailed memory, and its potency is reduced. Finley, Kim, and Mynatt (1979) reported that 91% of their students preferred playback and feedback immediately after videotaping.

The longer you delay the review session, the more likely it is that learners will have difficulty recalling some of the invisible events that are important to discuss, such as the diagnostic or therapeutic strategies they considered but did not act on during the encounter or the issues they considered pursuing but didn't. Passing thoughts and feelings—which are at risk of being lost if not discussed promptly—can be important clues to a learner's functioning. The crucial emotional elements of clinical exchanges (e.g., the learner's fears, discomforts, or feelings toward the patient) become progressively less accessible with the passage of time. Of course, you will gain access to these more subtle but fundamental aspects of clinical functioning only if you convey your own comfort in dealing with these matters and convince your learner that you have helpful observations to offer.

- **Develop a trusting relationship in which the learner feels comfortable taking the risks associated with self-assessment.**

Most learners feel vulnerable, at least initially, when reviewing video recordings of their work in the presence of teachers. If they are to identify and discuss both their strengths and weaknesses, they need to trust that we will use this information (particularly information about their weaknesses) to help them, not to hurt them.

Learners who have had prior experiences with teachers who were demeaning may be understandably cautious about being candid in their self-critiques. But if you are consistently supportive and respectful of them and provide constructive, helpful comments and feedback, most of them will let down their barriers and be honest with themselves and with you.

- **Ensure that you and the learner have privacy.**

An important element in helping learners feel comfortable being candid about their performance is holding review sessions in a room where the playback and your discussion cannot be heard by others.

- **Discuss the format for the review session, including your and the learner's roles.**

There are many ways to review video recordings of learners' work. If you and a learner are working alone and you want her to become effective at self-assessment, then it is likely that you will want her to take the lead in critiquing her performance while you focus on facilitating her self-assessment and providing her with your critique of her self-critique. Regardless of what roles you and the learner will each play, discuss these roles in advance so that each of you is clear about and agrees to the plans.

- **Be sure the learner understands why you will be trying to facilitate his or her own discoveries.**

Most learners are accustomed to being in the kinds of authoritarian educational environments we described in Chapter 1, in which teachers do things to and for learners. Few are accustomed to being partners who assume increasing responsibility for guiding their own learning. Learners who are products of authoritarian systems may become frustrated when you ask them questions rather than give them answers, when you serve as a facilitator rather than a purveyor of knowledge. When working with passive learners who are not accustomed to being active, self-directed learners, it is usually worthwhile to take time to help them understand why you use a collaborative approach—if that's what you do. Helping them make the transition is a vital investment in their long-term future and may take—and deserves—some time and effort.

- **Be sure that the learner knows how to use the video equipment.**

Find out about the learner's level of comfort and expertise in using the video equipment. If he has not operated it before, give him a chance to start and stop the tape, to fast-forward and rewind, and to use any available features, such as the still-frame capability to examine individual images. Remind the learner that he can replay segments multiple times and that he can turn off the sound and just study the picture.

- **Review the student's learning goals, exploring whether these goals have changed as a result of the event that was taped.**

Learning goals should not be treated as if they were engraved in stone. Unexpected events can provide challenges and opportunities that need to be addressed. For example, let's say that a student's original learning goal was to demonstrate an understanding of universal precautions while drawing blood from a patient. While she prepared to do this, however, the patient became very agitated, saying that he was afraid that he might get AIDS if she draws his blood. The student then was faced with trying to calm the patient. In reviewing a recording of this encounter with her supervisor, the student might well want to add to the agenda a review of how she handled the patient's fear and a discussion of effective strategies for managing similar encounters in the future.

- **If appropriate, propose additional goals and issues for the review session.**

Particularly if you observed the live encounter or have already reviewed the recording of that encounter, you may have additional issues or goals that you think should be dealt with in the review session. For example, the agreed-upon goal for a taped clinical encounter may have been for the student to tune in to the patient's nonverbal communication. While observing the live interaction, however, you recognized that the student was being subtly impatient and a little harsh. Although your observation takes you beyond the intended focus of the session, you might reasonably decide that your concern about the student's behavior with this patient cannot be overlooked. Before introducing your concern, it is important that you indicate your intention to modify the accepted plan. You might say something like, "As you look back at this interview, how do you react to the approach you took?" If necessary, you might add, "Are there any clues that you weren't fully comfortable with this patient?"

- **If necessary, negotiate and prioritize the learning goals for the review session.**

Reviews of video recordings enable you and the learner to study issues in depth. For example, the discussion of the opening moments of a patient encounter can sometimes trigger a discussion that lasts for 30 to 60 minutes. It is important, therefore, to set priorities for what you need to accomplish and to formulate a plan to assure that the important goals are accomplished.

- **Initially withhold your feedback, even positive feedback.**

As we discussed, initially withholding your feedback can be beneficial for both you and your learners. Doing so is particularly important with learners you don't know and learners who you think might not be candid about their views if they hear your feedback first.

- **Initially consider offering support rather than giving positive feedback.**

When a student handles a difficult situation well, many of us are understandably inclined to say something positive. You can avoid providing positive feedback prematurely while still conveying your sensitivity to the difficulty of the situation the learner has just faced and encouraging his self-critique. The following statement does not convey any judgment about the student's performance yet still expresses sensitivity and support: "That patient you just saw was quite a challenge. I must say, I would have had a difficult time dealing with his level of anger." Such a statement accomplishes several goals. It reveals your humanness and vulnerability, which contributes to your credibility and trustworthiness. It avoids the possibility of stifling the student's self-critique. And if the student experienced some discomfort with the patient's behavior and felt some embarrassment about his discomfort, your comment may increase his willingness to acknowledge his concerns.

This caution about avoiding premature feedback applies particularly to learners you do not yet know well. Postponing your views is less important if you know learners well and feel that they are sufficiently trusting of you that they are not likely to feel stifled by your opinions and feedback.

- **Be supportive throughout the review session.**

As just indicated, there is a difference between providing specific feedback and providing support. Throughout review sessions, don't hesitate to support learners and their efforts, particularly in nonjudgmental ways. Most learners thrive in supportive relationships, yet in some institutions learners get little or no support from their teachers.

- **Ask the learner to give a brief description of the recorded event.**

As we discussed, this task can help learners get started with the self-assessment process in the most straightforward, least stressful way. What they say and how they say it can give you helpful clues about their levels of comfort and insights about what transpired.

- **Invite the learner to summarize his or her critique before proceeding with a detailed review.**

Often, when asked to describe an encounter, learners also begin critiquing it. What they choose to talk about and how they initially assess their performance provides diagnostic information that can help you formulate a plan for guiding them in their further self-assessment.

- **Invite the learner to use the remote control to stop and start the playback.**

See Chapter 4.

- **Sit where you can easily see the learner and the monitor.**

The learners' nonverbal expressions and gestures while viewing the playback can give you clues about what they are thinking and feeling. When you sit so that you can easily see both the learner and the television screen, you can observe the learner, and you can nonverbally send him messages, such as a nod suggesting that he stop the tape and reflect on what took place in the preceding segment.

- **Decide how to review the tape.**

The way you review the tape depends largely on the learning goals. If, for example, the learner wants to focus on how she opens an interview and you agree, the review can be limited to the opening few moments of the interview. If she wants to study how she wraps up an interview, you can go immediately to the last few moments of the interview. If the learner wants to assess the extent to which she maintains a nonjudgmental posture throughout the interview, you can skip fairly rapidly through the tape, stopping only at events that help the learner look at how she presents herself to the patient. Or if a learner wants to look at the extent to which she uses open-ended questions, you can stop the tape at the end of each of her questions and analyze them.

You also need to decide and discuss in advance how you will proceed with the review. Typically, learners are encouraged to stop the tape every time they see or hear something they want to comment on or when they recognize a decision point. You can also signal learners to stop the tape whenever you have questions or comments.

- **Encourage the learner to stop the tape frequently.**

Most recordings are rich in learning opportunities. To take advantage of these opportunities, consider asking learners to stop the tape frequently and reflect in depth on what has occurred.

- **Use an open-ended, nonjudgmental approach when facilitating the learner's self-critique.**

As we discussed above, an open-ended, nonjudgmental approach can help learners express their thoughts and feelings in their own words. In addition to opening the interview with a statement like "Describe how it went," consider some of the following questions for use during the review:

- What were you thinking?
- What were you feeling?
- How do you think the patient was feeling?
- What did the patient seem to want from you?

- How would you describe that last exchange with the patient?
- Was there anything you wanted to say or do but didn't?
- How would you describe the approach you've been using?

- **Use verbal and nonverbal encouragement to explore the learner's thoughts and feelings further.**

In patient care, verbal and nonverbal encouragement can help patients present their stories in more depth. In critique sessions, similar encouragement can help learners more fully express themselves. Nods and smiles can help, as can short questions and phrases such as:

- What else do you think is happening?
- Anything else?
- Please go on.

- **Even if you signal the learner to stop the tape, whenever appropriate, begin by inviting his or her self-assessment.**

Particularly when the learner is new to the process of self-assessment, when you want to stop and discuss a segment of the tape, consider first asking the learner to comment. For example, consider saying something like, "Did you see anything here you'd like to comment on?" Or ask an open-ended question like, "How were you feeling at this point?"

- **Be sure the learner identifies both strengths and deficiencies.**

Too often critique sessions are seen as times to focus on learners' deficiencies. Although it is important to identify areas that learners need to work on, it is equally important to identify what they are doing well. Identifying and discussing learners' strengths and capabilities helps them realize they are making progress. The formal education of health professionals is often arduous. In the midst of all of the new knowledge they must assimilate and the skills they must master, many students feel overwhelmed and discouraged, losing track of the progress they have already made.

In addition, learners might be unaware of their strengths, resulting in the possibility they may drop important approaches and strategies from their repertoires. And it is far easier to accept discussions of deficiencies when they are balanced with a recognition of strengths.

- **Review segments multiple times when appropriate.**

When examining video recordings, take advantage of the ability to review segments multiple times, perhaps focusing on different issues or perspectives with each playback.

- **Consider turning the audio off when reviewing nonverbal behavior.**

Nonverbal communication can often best be examined by turning off the audio so that you and the learner are not distracted by what is being said. You can invite learners to look at and reflect on their own gestures, postures, and facial expressions, perhaps trying to interpret them from a patient's perspective. You can also ask them to observe and try to interpret the patient's nonverbal behavior. An exercise you might find helpful is reviewing with a group of students a tape that none of them has seen before. On first viewing, ask them to try to interpret the verbal and emotional content of the exchange. Then replay the tape with the sound switched on.

- **Provide your feedback throughout the session, as appropriate.**

After listening to your learners' self-assessments, add additional observations, insights, opinions, and thoughts that you think will be helpful to the learner. The dominant need of most learners is help in refining their capacity for self-critique, so your feedback should usually concentrate on this area (see Chapter 7).

- **Invite the learner to summarize what he or she has learned.**

At the close of review sessions, ask learners to identify what they have learned during the review session. In particular, ask them to examine the extent to which they achieved their learning goals.

- **Invite the learner to identify new learning goals that emerged during the review session.**

Learners should be encouraged to take any deficiencies and problems they identified and turn them into learning goals. For example, if a learner realized that she kept her head buried in the patient's chart during much of the interview, she might set a goal for future interviews of maintaining good eye contact with patients. A learner who was confronted during the review session with the limitations of his knowledge (e.g., his uncertainty about the signs and symptoms of multiple sclerosis) might set becoming familiar with that information as his goal.

- **Discuss the learner's self-assessment.**

Particularly if one of the explicit goals was for the learner to enhance her capacity for self-assessment, take time at the end of the review session to ask her to critique the assessment she did of herself during the review session. If you have feedback you'd like to add to the learner's critique of her critique, do so.

- **Consider saving some or all of the recordings.**

It is difficult for learners to keep track of their progress over time. Saving all or some of the recordings made of learners' work enables you and your learners to study their progress over weeks, months, or even years. Learners who feel that they aren't making any headway can find it gratifying to compare their awkward efforts in their early recordings with their more competent efforts in more recent recordings. And if you and/or your learners need to evaluate and make formal judgments about their progress during a clinical learning experience, you have video documents to which you can turn.

Videotapes are so inexpensive that the easiest way for learners to create video logs of their work is to purchase their own tapes and use them for recording each of their performances. (Several events can often be recorded on one tape.) Learners can keep their tapes in their possession, or you can keep them at the school or program after developing a mechanism for ensuring that only appropriate people (e.g., you, the learners, and the course coordinator) have access to the them.

- **Encourage the learner to write a brief summary of the session.**

Writing a summary can help learners further consolidate their thinking. The process of writing might also stimulate them to make further discoveries. Consider asking learners to submit their summaries to you so that you can review them and then discuss them together.

- **Encourage learners to keep journals.**

Journals can be excellent tools for helping learners reflect on their learning experiences, including sessions in which they review video recordings of their work. Reilly (1958) described journal writing as "a dialogue with the self, representing a record of the student's feelings, reactions, attitudes, perceptions, and activities in the clinical environment."

Appendix 6.1

Self-Checklist for Educators: Using Video for Guiding Learner Self-Assessments

Did I . . .

- ☐ Review the recording with the learner as soon as possible after it was made?
- ☐ Develop a trusting relationship in which the learner felt comfortable risking a self-assessment?
- ☐ Ensure that the learner and I had privacy?
- ☐ Discuss the format for the review session, including the learner's role and my role?
- ☐ Make sure the learner understood why I wanted to facilitate his or her own discoveries?
- ☐ Ensure that the learner knew how to use the video equipment?
- ☐ Review the student's learning goals, exploring whether they had changed as a result of the patient encounter?
- ☐ Propose additional goals and issues, if appropriate?
- ☐ Negotiate and prioritize the learning goals, if appropriate?
- ☐ Initially withhold my feedback, even positive feedback, particularly with learners with whom I have not yet built a solid, trusting relationship?
- ☐ Show support for the learner throughout the session?
- ☐ Ask the learner to give a brief description of the recorded event?
- ☐ Invite the learner to summarize his or her self-critique before proceeding with a detailed review?
- ☐ Invite the learner to use the remote control to stop and start the playback?
- ☐ Sit where I could easily see the learner and the monitor?
- ☐ Decide with the learner how to review the tape?
- ☐ Encourage the learner to stop the tape frequently?
- ☐ Use an open-ended, nonjudgmental approach when facilitating the learner's self-critique?
- ☐ Use verbal and nonverbal encouragement to further explore the learner's thoughts and feelings?
- ☐ First invite the learner's self-assessment, even when I signaled the learner to stop the tape?
- ☐ Ensure that the learner identified both strengths and deficiencies?

Appendix 6.1 *(continued)*

Did I . . .

- ☐ Review segments of the tape multiple times when appropriate?
- ☐ Suggest that the learner turn the audio off when reviewing nonverbal behavior?
- ☐ Invite the learner to summarize what he or she learned?
- ☐ Invite the learner to identify new learning goals that emerged during the review session?
- ☐ Discuss the learner's self-assessment?
- ☐ Consider saving some or all of the recording?
- ☐ Encourage/ask the learner to write a brief summary of the review session?

From: Westberg, J., Jason, H. *Teaching Creatively with Video: Fostering Reflection, Communication and Other Clinical Skills,* New York: Springer Publishing Co., 1994.

Appendix 6.2

Self-Checklist for Health Professionals: Opening of Interview

Key:

Y = Yes N = No NA = Not Applicable

Circle the appropriate letters. Use space under items to write specific comments, including examples of what was done effectively and ineffectively. (Use over as needed.)

Did I . . .

Y N NA 1. Greet the patient in a friendly, attentive, respectful manner?

Describe:

Y N NA 2. Attend to introductions of myself and the patient?

Describe:

Y N NA 3. Help put the patient at ease (e.g., engage in transitional small talk)?

Describe:

Y N NA 4. Use an open-ended approach (e.g., begin the interview and new topics with open-ended questions)?

Describe:

Y N NA 5. Verbally and nonverbally communicate attentiveness and openness?

Describe:

Y N NA 6. Give the patient an adequate opportunity to identify and discuss his or her reasons for today's visit?

Describe:

Y N NA 7. Find out what the patient hoped to accomplish at this visit (e.g., have questions answered, get a prescription)?

Describe:

Other comments:

From: Westberg, J., Jason, H. *Teaching Creatively with Video: Fostering Reflection, Communication and Other Clinical Skills,* New York: Springer Publishing Co., 1994.

CHAPTER 7

Using Video for Providing Constructive Feedback

As we discussed in the previous chapter, helping learners become effective at self-critique is one of our fundamental tasks. A companion task, especially when students are first learning or substantially refining complex skills, is providing them with appropriate feedback. In the early stages of learning new skills, students typically do not have a full, clear picture of what they need to know and do. They are unconsciously incompetent. Also, when trying to make a major shift in the way they function (e.g., moving from being authoritarian to being collaborative in their dealings with patients), they can usually profit substantially from feedback. Indeed, since becoming and continuing to grow as a health professional is a lifelong task, we and our students should have regular access to constructive feedback throughout our careers, much as professional athletes and performers do throughout their careers.

As we discussed in Chapter 1, effective feedback can accelerate and facilitate learning. Without feedback, mistakes can go uncorrected and bad habits can be consolidated. Conversely, if learners don't receive feedback on their strengths, they are at risk of discontinuing some of their desirable behaviors. Without feedback, learners may make inaccurate assumptions, both negative and positive, about their work.

Providing constructive feedback, particularly negative constructive feedback, is one of the toughest challenges facing us as teachers. As we discuss here, video can make this task far easier and enable us to be more effective.

In this chapter, we

- discuss reasons for using video in providing feedback
- discuss some of the issues related to preparing for and providing feedback to learners
- provide specific suggestions for (1) preparing for giving feedback, and (2) giving feedback to learners.

REASONS FOR USING VIDEO IN PROVIDING FEEDBACK

Using video recordings of your learners at work in clinical settings gives you and them the unique opportunity to jointly observe their work. Also, as we discussed in Chapter 6, you and the learner have an objective record of the event, so you don't need to spend valuable time during supervisory sessions trying to reconstruct what transpired.

You can conduct supervisory reviews of prior events in much greater depth than would otherwise be possible.

Video gives you and learners access to rich material that is not otherwise available, such as the learners' nonverbal communications. It gives you access to the myriad details that are quickly lost from memory when events are over. And video provides access to the learners' invisible processes as they reflect aloud and critique their performance while reviewing the videotapes.

You can review the recording when, and as often as, you need to.

In real life, you can't manipulate time. With video, though, you can shift the time when an event is supervised, review an event multiple times, play it back in slow motion, and freeze its motion. In sum, you can do whatever it takes to enhance your grasp of what was going on so that you can give helpful guidance to learners.

You can illustrate and reinforce your feedback with specific segments from the recording.

Much of the feedback that learners receive is abstract and minimally communicative. Letter grades, such as A, B, or F, and words like *excellent*, *good*, and *poor* are abstractions that convey no information about what learners did well or poorly or what further steps they should take. Statements such as "You did a good job," might cause learners to feel good for a moment, but they provide no guidance toward further improvement. Similarly, negative statements, such as "That was a lousy interview," don't tell learners where they are deficient or what they need to work on.

Constructive feedback is as specific as possible. When giving feedback to students, we need to paint pictures of what we are saying and provide concrete examples. Video recordings of our learners' work enable us to *show* them what we are talking about. If we are concerned because a student failed to introduce himself to a patient, we can show her an image of her behavior and its consequences. Having this capacity to show events to learners is especially helpful when it is difficult to put events or our feedback into words.

ISSUES AND CONSIDERATIONS

Learners need feedback throughout courses and CLEs.

Once pilots set a course for a particular destination and begin their flight, they focus their attention on a continuing stream of information (feedback) so they can make any needed midcourse corrections. Once students set learning goals, they also need continuous feedback so they can make appropriate midcourse corrections and not go off in unproductive or counterproductive directions. Unfortunately, in too many schools and programs in the health professions, learners are given little or no feedback of educational consequence. The grades and comments they receive at the end of courses or CLEs are seldom more than minimally helpful and arrive too late for learners to make midcourse corrections. Periodic reviews of video recordings of their work throughout courses and CLEs can provide learners with vivid, powerful feedback that can help guide their learning.

Learners who have had hurtful experiences with feedback are not likely to want more feedback.

At some time in our lives, most of us have had teachers deliver feedback to us in inappropriate, harsh, hurtful ways. For some learners, such negative experiences with feedback dominate their formal education. Understandably, such learners are likely to avoid additional sources of feedback whenever they can. When doing self-critiques of their work during supervisory sessions, for example, these learners are likely to withhold negative information about themselves until they are convinced that they can genuinely trust us.

Some teachers have had no models of constructive feedback to emulate.

During workshops and courses, we have asked thousands of health professions educators about their experiences with receiving feedback during their formal education. Most report receiving little or no truly constructive feedback. Too many report that the limited amount of personal feedback they received was mainly unpleasant, poorly timed, insensitive, hurtful, and ultimately not helpful.

Few if any teachers intend to give feedback in harmful ways, yet too often people do to others what was done to them. They treat others as they have been treated. A well-recognized, tragic illustration of this phenomenon is the perpetuation of child abuse. A high proportion of parents who abuse children were themselves abused when they were children (Helfer & Kempe, 1976; McNeese & Hebeles, 1977). Teachers who don't have positive models to emulate or who have had painful experiences with feedback, or both, are at risk of replicating their own experiences for their students. They need to reflect on those experiences and work especially hard to ensure that they break the cycle; that they provide feedback in helpful, constructive ways.

Some teachers and learners fear that feedback might damage their relationships with each other.

Ende (1983), in a helpful article on feedback, described the notion of "vanishing feedback," a concept from the field of personnel management that he suggests applies equally to medical education. Ende said that teachers who are well intentioned in their commitment to the need for feedback but uneasy about the impact their feedback may have on their trainees tend to talk around the learner's problems, use indirect statements, or speak in generalities and abstractions, essentially obfuscating their evaluation messages. Some examples of vanishing feedback: "For your level of training, you did fine." "You seem to be making satisfactory progress." "You were clearly trying during your time on this service." Such observations convey nothing that contributes to the learner's growth.

Many learners, in turn, fear that any effort they might make to elicit more meaningful feedback may result in their receiving unpleasant, unwelcome information. They support and reinforce their teacher's avoidance of what should be a central issue between them. The result in many instructional encounters, despite the best of intentions, is that little of real value gets transmitted or received.

Giving constructive feedback, especially negative feedback, can be genuinely challenging. Life and conventional education provide little if any preparation for exercising this complex set of skills. Yet providing such feedback is undoubtedly one of the central elements of helpful teaching.

When you offer negative feedback to learners, you take a risk. You are opening the possibility of incurring the learners' complaints, anger, even retaliation. But if your feedback is constructive and you are able to convey your desire to be helpful, your relationships with learners are likely to deepen, not diminish. If learners invite your feedback, you can usually interpret the invitation as an enormous compliment to you, implying that you have achieved one of the central tasks of teaching: you have earned your learner's trust!

Learners vary in their levels of receptivity to feedback.

Some learners are eager for feedback, even invite it. Others avoid it. A multitude of factors contribute to learners' varying levels of receptivity, including their sense of self-worth and self-confidence and their prior experiences with feedback. Because of these differences it's important to assess each learner's readiness for feedback and not have a standardized approach to all learners, as if they were all alike.

An individual's receptivity to feedback can vary according to the circumstances.

Learner receptivity to feedback can be influenced by both recent and past events. If a student has just emerged from a traumatic experience with a patient or recently received a large dose of negative feedback, he will probably not be open to much additional feedback at this time. When deciding when to give feedback and how much to offer, we need to be sensitive to the learner's recent experiences and current emotional and intellectual state.

We need to create environments in which learners invite feedback from others.

If our learners are to continue to grow as professionals after they graduate, they need to be open to and even invite feedback from others. They are most likely to have this openness if they have had repeated positive experiences with seeking and receiving constructive feedback during their formal education. Supervisory sessions present us with the challenge of consistently providing learners with opportunities for safely seeking and getting helpful feedback.

There are several potentially helpful sources of feedback for learners.

Besides yourself and other teachers, there are other potential sources of feedback, including the learners' peers (see Chapter 8), simulated and real patients (see Chapter 9), and other health professionals.

SUGGESTIONS

PREPARING FOR GIVING FEEDBACK

- **Reflect on your own experiences with receiving feedback.**

Because of our human tendency to treat others as we have been treated, it can be helpful to reflect on our own experiences as recipients of feedback. If you are not currently accustomed to receiving feedback, consider asking a colleague to critique your teaching or patient care to see if that reawakens your feelings about being on the receiving end of feedback. Some questions to reflect on:

- What are some of your most memorable experiences receiving feedback? How would you describe them?

- How would you characterize your helpful experiences with feedback?
- How would you characterize your negative experiences with feedback?
- How would you describe the way you currently give feedback to others, particularly learners?
- How would you characterize the focus of the feedback you typically give to others?
- How aware do you tend to be of the *process* and *content* components of your learners' performance when you give feedback?

- **Consider reviewing the learner's recording yourself, prior to reviewing it with the learner.**

If you have time, it can be helpful to review video recordings of learners by yourself prior to reviewing them with your learners. This is particularly true if you are new to the instructional strategy of reviewing recordings with learners or if you are focusing on some issues that are relatively new for you. Such previews will give you a chance to gather your thoughts and set your goals and priorities in advance of your meeting with the learner.

- **Consider writing down your reactions, linked to the appropriate counter numbers.**

Sometimes it can be helpful for you and the learner to play back an event in its entirety before playing it back and stopping it frequently to discuss its details. Whether you watch a playback alone in advance of your meeting with a learner or watch it in its entirety with the learner, make notes of locations on the tape to which you would like to return during the detailed review with the learner. You can do this by setting the counter to "00" at the beginning of the taped event. Then, during the playback, when you come to a place you would like to review with the learner, make a note of the counter number and the issue you want to explore with the learner.

- **Be clear about the special needs of your learners.**

In patient care, the kinds of feedback we provide to patients and the ways we provide that feedback differ according to the special needs of each patient. Likewise, learners' levels of readiness, their self-concepts, and their self-knowledge are among the factors to consider when giving feedback. Providing individualized feedback requires knowledge of our learners that we can acquire in part by inviting and listening carefully to their self-assessments.

GIVING FEEDBACK TO LEARNERS

A fundamental task in creating an environment in which learners welcome, even invite, feedback is taking steps to build trust-based relationships. Also, as we discussed in Chapter 6, we recommend that you encourage your learners to take the lead in critiquing their performance and that you facilitate their reflection and self-assessment—help them make their own discoveries. Among other things, this approach gives them practice in being reflective; gives them the dignity of identifying their own areas of need; and provides you with important diagnostic information about your learners, including clues as to whether your hypotheses about their performance—and the associated feedback you want them to have—is on track.

When you discuss the format of the review session with your learners, they also need to be aware that you will be providing them with feedback. You can explain though that some of the points you intend to make may well be points they will make first when they assess their performance.

- **When you see an event on the tape that you want to discuss, signal the learner to stop the tape if she or he hasn't already done so.**

Sometimes simply signaling learners to stop the tape will precipitate their reflection: "Yeah, I saw what I was doing there but was waiting to see if I kept on doing it." At other times when you request learners to stop the tape, they will be puzzled. At that point you might say something like "Did you see anything you'd like to comment on?" If they still didn't see anything, you might suggest that they review the segment again. Sometimes it helps to give them a clue; for example, "What about the kinds of questions you were asking?" or "What about the way you were sitting?"

It's important not to get into a protracted game of Guess What I'm Thinking? But if learners understand why you are trying to facilitate their self-discovery rather than giving them answers, they are likely to appreciate what you are doing. If learners aren't making important discoveries on their own or if you don't feel that your feedback will interfere with their openness in expressing their views, provide your feedback directly, keeping in mind some of the suggestions below.

- **When possible, link your feedback to the agreed-upon goals.**

Learners are likely to be most receptive to your feedback if you connect it to what you and they agreed were their goals: "You said that you would like to focus on presenting information to patients in clear, nontechnical language. Let's look at how that went today." On the other hand, instructional goals or priorities need not be treated as unduly constraining. If important, unanticipated issues emerge during the event that was recorded, try remaining flexible. Consider raising these new issues, but acknowledge that you are deviating from the original plan.

- **Focus on the learner's behavior and performance, rather than making sweeping judgments about him or her as a person.**

Telling learners that they are incompetent, inadequate, insensitive, or anything else that categorizes them as people and causes them to feel attacked is usually counterproductive to fostering trust, collaboration, or growth. Even positive labels, such as *brilliant* and *wonderful*, typically aren't helpful. Labeling people can be tempting because it can appear to simplify our lives. Most people, however, are enormously complex and can't and shouldn't be reduced to labels. In addition, once learners have been labeled, there can be a tendency for teachers to perceive only those components of the learners' behavior that justify or contradict the assigned labels.

In addition, although people enjoy hearing positive labels and dislike or resent negative ones, neither contributes to the learners' understandings of which specific components of their behavior they need to change and which they should preserve. As we explain more fully below, in place of such labels, descriptive language is usually most helpful. For example:

- In place of *insensitive*: "Mr. Smith seemed quite upset by the way you explained his condition."
- In place of *bright*: "Your insights into the reasons Ms. Brown is having trouble giving up cigarettes go well beyond what I usually expect from a student at your level of education."

Giving specific descriptions and objective evidence, particularly of negative behaviors, accomplishes at least two goals. It reduces the possibility that learners will become defensive and resistant, reasserting their right to sustain their current behaviors and discrediting your advice rather than becoming open to considering and trying some alternative behaviors. And it directs learners to explicit actions and habits that can be modified.

- **Be as specific as possible, referring the learner to events on the tape when possible.**

As we just explained, labeling learners can be hurtful. Even making general statements to learners about their behavior usually isn't helpful to them. Statements such as "That was a wonderful interview" and "That was an incompetent exam" don't give learners sufficient information to guide them in changing their behavior. General positive statements don't tell learners what they did well and should continue doing. General negative statements don't tell learners where they are deficient and what they need to work on.

When providing feedback, it is generally most helpful to point to concrete examples. The video recording provides a unique opportunity to show learners what you are talking about. It can provide them with objective, tangible evidence.

- **Whenever possible, begin your feedback with a positive observation.**

Usually, there is something positive that can be said about a learner's effort, achievement, self-assessment, or openness. Try finding something good to say after learners' self-assessments, while avoiding the pattern of having your opening positive remarks become so automatic and perfunctory that your learners anticipate and dismiss them. Most learners hear so few positive observations about their performance that making a habit of starting out on a positive tone can be encouraging and helpful.

- **Be careful not to follow every positive observation with a *but* . . . and a negative observation.**

Too many teachers who open their critiques with positive comments fall into the habit of next saying something like, "...but you did make a number of mistakes." Students quickly detect this pattern and soon begin disregarding the opening commendations while waiting for the other shoe to drop.

Learners do need to be aware of both their strengths and deficiencies, but we generally do best by linking them with the conjunction *and*, rather than the conjunction *but*. This distinction might appear to be trivial, but the word *and* is consistent with the notion that we all have both strengths and deficiences. When learners hear positive comments followed by the word *but*, many of them conclude that their deficiencies far overshadow their strengths.

- **Give learners a language with which to reflect on their performance.**

Some learners don't know how to think or talk about their performance. If they are learning a technical skill, and particularly if they are aware of the steps involved in using that skill, they can usually decide whether they have taken the needed steps. Many learners, however, need help in developing ways of thinking about less straightforward issues. For example, when reflecting on interactions with patients it can be helpful for them to understand concepts such as *open-ended* versus *closed* questions and *nonjudgmental* versus *judgmental* approaches. When you provide feedback, you can introduce and use the concepts that are relevant to the skills learners are trying to acquire, and you can encourage them to use these concepts in their self-critiques.

- **When your feedback is subjective, label it as such.**

This principle in the use of feedback is parallel to the increasingly common approach in patient record keeping in which subjective clinical findings are labeled as such. The instructional setting has no equivalent to the many laboratory tests available in the clinical setting, so a higher proportion of instructional conclusions are inescapably subjective. Even our best efforts at being objective in our assessments are at risk of being tinged by our human tendency to be subjective in our selective perception and interpretation of events. The video recording can help us be more objective. In fact we might even modify our assessment after reviewing segments of a tape. But even though we can review an event multiple times, our interpretation of much of what we see is still prone to subjectivity.

The most direct technique for acknowledging the subjectivity of our feedback is using "I" statements. For example, instead of presenting assertions as though they were unarguably true (e.g., "You were repeatedly preoccupied when the patient tried to ..."), consider statements such as "It looks to me as though you were ..." By labeling subjective feedback as deriving from your point of view, you imply that your feedback is not necessarily the final word, and you invite learners to consider challenging your judgment—an important step in their professional maturation. Acknowledging the subjectivity of our observations and hypotheses enhances our credibility as teachers, increases the likelihood that learners will be trusting and receptive toward our contributions, and provides learners with a model worth emulating.

- **Avoid overloading the learner with feedback.**

When giving feedback to learners, it can be tempting to convey all of our observations and thoughts. It is usually best, however, to squelch that desire. Most learners, especially those in the early stages of their development, can deal with only one topic at a time. Many can deal with only a few issues in the course of an entire supervisory session. Partly, feedback from a teacher—especially feedback that has negative components—can feel fairly heavy. Also, issues that seem simple and straightforward to experienced health professionals can appear quite complicated to neophytes, who need time to fully understand and integrate new information and views, especially about their own behavior.

Hopefully, you will have more than one video review session with each learner you supervise. As with patients, continuity of care with students can lead to better understandings of their backgrounds, characteristics, and needs. Also, when you anticipate having multiple encounters with patients or students, you do not have to do or say everything in any one encounter.

- **Be supportive when providing feedback.**

If you can convey unwavering support for learners, even while expressing your concerns about a problem that has emerged in the review process, your contributions are likely to be heard, valued, and assimilated. If learners perceive you as indifferent or disdainful rather than supportive, your feedback will be less helpful than it could have been.

- **Remember that both *what* you say and *how* you say it are important.**

Much of our discussion in this chapter has been on *what* to say to learners when providing feedback. Much of the message—some researchers say *most* of the message—in verbal communication comes not from our words but from the subtext or meta-message: the tone, pacing, volume, and body language that accompany our words (Tannen, 1986). A critical challenge is ensuring that we are genuinely supportive of each of our learners, that our words are unambiguous in conveying that support, and that our nonverbal communication is fully coherent with our words. Probably the most valuable step we can take in achieving these goals is videotaping and reviewing our work as supervisors, alone or with a trusted colleague, focusing on these issues.

- **Invite the learner's reaction to your feedback.**

As we've mentioned, the supervisory process should be a dialogue, not a monologue. When we simply drop observations and comments on learners without inviting their reactions, we risk not being heard, being misunderstood, and having an impact that we didn't intend.

After giving feedback to learners you can facilitate their reactions to your feedback with phrases or questions such as:

- Well, that's what I observed. What is your perception of what happened?
- What's your reaction to my feedback?

Inviting the learner's reaction accomplishes several purposes:

- You can determine whether the learner heard and understood what you said.
- You can get clues to the learner's readiness for and receptivity to the feedback you provided.
- You may get clues to the learner's general readiness for and receptivity to feedback of any sort.
- The learner can challenge or clear up any misconceptions you might have.

What you learn can guide your next steps. If, for example, the learner is defensive, you may need to stop and explore the roots of her defensiveness. On the other hand, if the learner is open to your feedback, you might want to jointly explore your observations and comments in greater depth.

- **Help the learner turn negative feedback into constructive challenges.**

Delivering negative observations in ways that help learners feel constructively challenged, not demeaned or assaulted, is challenging. Usually, the key to success with this demanding task, as we indicated above, is linking your feedback to previously agreed-upon goals. If the learner has already expressed his commitment to a particular goal, then your challenge is helping him translate the negative feedback into constructive ways of reaching his goal.

> You said that you want to include attention to prevention issues in your encounters with patients. As we just discussed, you weren't able to do that in this interaction. What steps could you take next time to be sure that you include prevention issues?

On the other hand, if your feedback does not pertain to the learner's goals or values, your challenge might first be to help convince the learner of the importance of your feedback or suggestion. For example, if you feel that patients should be helped to be active partners in their care but your learner uses a more authoritarian approach to patients, you might first need to help the learner understand and become committed to a more collaborative approach to care.

- **Encourage the learner to invite your feedback and to let you know when it is difficult to hear your feedback.**

Ideally, learners will come to trust you and value your feedback so highly that they will genuinely welcome your observations. Do not expect such an attitude to emerge quickly, but do work toward this goal. Also, invite learners to let you know when they want you to postpone your feedback. For example, if you sense the learner is feeling stressed, you might say something like "I have some feedback for you. First, tell me if this is a good time for you." If you have earned some measure of trust from this learner, you will likely get a straight answer.

- **Provide follow-up to your feedback whenever appropriate.**

As we've indicated, feedback should not be dumped on learners. You may find it helpful to think of feedback as the equivalent of a potent therapeutic intervention in patient care. You would not, for example, give a beta blocker to a patient without careful follow-up on his progress.

After giving feedback to learners, particularly negative feedback, your task is far from done. You must still ensure that learners develop a plan for dealing with the identified problems or deficiencies. Also, you may need to arrange a way to work with them in monitoring their progress.

Little if any meaningful change in human behavior occurs as the result of a single brief intervention. Providing for follow-up can reinforce and ensure the lasting, positive outcome your feedback is meant to achieve. It can also help avoid any of the undesirable potential consequences of providing feedback.

- **Make notes that can guide your next interaction with the learner.**

To assure that you do not forget what happened in the supervisory session and the issues you want to pursue in future encounters, consider making some notes for yourself during or as soon after the session as possible.

Appendix 7.1

Self-Checklist for Educators: Giving Feedback to Learners

Do I . . .

- ☐ Establish and maintain a climate of trust in which learners welcome, even invite, my feedback?
- ☐ Make sure learners understand that I will provide feedback to them during review sessions—and how?
- ☐ Signal the learner to stop the tape if she or he hasn't already done so, when I see an event on the tape that I want to discuss?
- ☐ Begin by inviting the learner's self-assessment?
- ☐ As much as possible, help learners make their own discoveries?
- ☐ Link my feedback to the agreed-upon goals when possible?
- ☐ Focus on learners' behaviors and performances, rather than making judgments about them as people?
- ☐ Try to be as specific as possible, referring the learner to events in the tape when possible?
- ☐ When possible, begin my feedback with positive observations?
- ☐ Avoid following my positive observations with but... and a negative observation?
- ☐ Give learners a language with which to reflect on their performance?
- ☐ When my feedback is subjective, label it as such?
- ☐ Avoid overloading learners with feedback?
- ☐ Demonstrate support for learners when providing feedback?
- ☐ Attend to both *what* I say and *how* I say it?
- ☐ Invite the learner's reaction to my feedback?
- ☐ Help learners turn negative feedback into constructive challenges?
- ☐ Encourage learners to invite my feedback and to let me know when it is difficult to hear my feedback?
- ☐ Provide follow-up to my feedback when appropriate?
- ☐ Take notes on the supervisory session to guide future encounters with the learner?

From: Westberg, J., Jason, H. *Teaching Creatively with Video: Fostering Reflection, Communication and Other Clinical Skills,* New York: Springer Publishing Co., 1994.

Appendix 7.2

Evaluation Form for Educators: Opening of Interview

Key:

Y = Yes   N = No   NA = Not Applicable

Circle the appropriate letters. Use space under items to write specific comments, including examples of what was done effectively and ineffectively. (Use over as needed.)

Did the learner . . .

Y N NA 1. Greet the patient in a friendly, attentive, respectful manner?

Describe:

Y N NA 2. Attend to introductions?

Describe:

Y N NA 3. Help put the patient at ease (e.g., engage in transitional small talk)?

Describe:

Y N NA 4. Use an open-ended approach (e.g., begin the interview and new topics with open-ended questions)?

Describe:

Y N NA 5. Verbally and nonverbally communicate attentiveness and openness?

Describe:

Y N NA 6. Give the patient an adequate opportunity to identify and discuss his or her reasons for today's visit?

Describe:

Y N NA 7. Find out what the patient hoped to accomplish with this visit (e.g., have questions answered, get a prescription)?

Describe:

Other comments:

From: Westberg, J., Jason, H. *Teaching Creatively with Video: Fostering Reflection, Communication and Other Clinical Skills,* New York: Springer Publishing Co., 1994.

CHAPTER 8

Helping Learners Use Video for Peer Review

In most educational programs in the health professions insufficient attention is given to peer teaching and learning, particularly in preclinical courses. Even in the clinical years, where there is a long history of teaching by near-peers, this strategy is often used less than optimally. When learners are asked to supervise the work of more junior learners (in essence, to serve as teachers), they are rarely helped to prepare for this important task. For that matter, few educators in the health professions, particularly in medicine, have had formal preparation for their instructional tasks (Jason & Westberg, 1982).

To provide high-quality care, health professionals need to work collaboratively, and they need to foster each other's growth. As greater attention is paid to continuing quality improvement, more professionals will need to critique their own work and the work of their peers. When we give our learners opportunities for peer review during their basic professional education, we are equipping them for their future.

Video is a unique and powerful tool for enhancing the process of peer review and other peer teaching and learning. Peer review can be based on events that peers witness together (e.g., students can observe a peer doing a procedure and then review a tape of that event as a group) or solely on video recordings of events that took place at an earlier time.

In this chapter, we

- examine reasons for learners to review each other's work
- identify and discuss reasons for using video for peer review

- examine some issues and considerations related to peer review
- provide suggestions for (1) preparing learners for peer review, and (2) facilitating peer review, using video.

REASONS FOR LEARNERS TO REVIEW EACH OTHER'S WORK

People who have recently acquired new competencies can be helpful guides.

When you need directions to a restaurant in a city that is unfamiliar to you, a person from that city who frequently travels to that restaurant may not be your best advisor. You are often best off asking someone who recently found his way to that restaurant for the first time. The expert can easily find his way, but he may not be able to convey clearly what you should do. When negotiating that trip, the expert no longer thinks about what he's doing. He proceeds so automatically that he may well have forgotten about some of the decisions that need to be made along the way, such as the fact that a tricky double turn must be negotiated when exiting from the main highway. He probably has put away or misplaced his map because he no longer needs it. On the other hand, the person who recently found his way to the restaurant for the first time is likely to still have a map handy and to be acutely aware of any confusing decisions that must be made. Translated into terms we've used throughout this book, you will be better off getting your advice from someone who is consciously competent than from someone who has become unconsciously competent.

Similarly, seasoned health professionals are not always the best ones to give learners detailed instructions about how to gain some capabilities that have long since become second nature for them. Unless people make an effort to remember important details and recapture their learning history, they are at risk of becoming unconsciously competent. On the other hand, the learners' peers or near-peers who have recently mastered new capabilities are like the person who recently found his way to a restaurant for the first time. The experiences of the learners' peers, including the sources of confusion and other difficulties they faced, are still fresh in their minds. They can readily understand and anticipate many problems that tend to be faced by beginners.

Collaborative efforts can enhance learning and achievement.

Many of us have witnessed the power of collaborative efforts. Learners can be effective tutors of each other, and they often learn in the process of helping their peers. Also, when learners share their knowledge, experience, and perspectives as they work on common tasks, the products of their efforts can be richer than the products of individuals. For example, peers can collectively come up with a variety of ways to approach challenging patient situations. In their meta-analysis of 122 studies of the relative effectiveness of cooperation, competition, and individualistic goal structures in promoting achievement and productivity in learners, Johnson and Maruyama (1981) found that cooperation is superior to competition and individualistic efforts in promoting achievement and productivity.

Students need to learn the peer review and consultation skills they will need as professionals.

With the increasing emphasis on continuous quality improvement, professionals are being called on to function as members of teams that routinely reflect on their work, identify issues that need attention, and work out strategies for addressing these issues. Professionals are asked to approach these tasks in a spirit of cooperation and support, rather than in an atmosphere of blaming.

To be skilled at peer review, learners need a thorough understanding of the clinical capabilities they are reviewing. They also need to understand the teaching-learning process so they can take the steps that will be most helpful to their colleagues.

Being reflective about their peers' performance can help learners be more reflective about their own work.

The process of teaching can be a helpful learning experience for those who teach. For example, when a student tries to help a peer think through a complex problem, she is likely to need to clarify her own thinking. When she notices that a peer is ignoring a patient while doing a procedure, she is likely to wonder if she occasionally does the same thing.

REASONS FOR USING VIDEO FOR PEER REVIEW

In real clinical settings, it's usually not possible for all peers to observe each other.

In classroom settings with simulated challenges, it is usually easy for learners to observe as their peers solve problems, do procedures on models or manikins, or counsel simulated patients. In real clinical situations, it is typically difficult or inappropriate for learners to observe as their peers examine patients, do procedures, and talk with patients. Video recordings of these events enable learners to witness their peers engaged in these activities.

Even if peers directly witness the event they are to critique, they may not notice or remember all of the key issues.

Seasoned football fans who watch 15 seconds of a game are likely to provide you with far more information about what was going on than are new fans who observe the same 15-second segment. The seasoned fans have seen so many plays that they can quickly grasp the big picture of what is going on (e.g., that the play is a quarterback sneak) and can simultaneously focus on the details (e.g., that an unusually good block by the center was the key to the play's success). On the other hand, the new sports fans might pick up some of the event (e.g., who has the ball and where he's heading) but not perceive the many details of this complex moment. In De Groot's frequently cited study (1946), grand master chess players were able to recall positions of pieces on the chessboard more accurately than were players with less knowledge and experience.

Like seasoned sports fans and chess players, experienced teachers can usually perceive a good deal when observing learners engaged in complex events, such as a clinical encounter, because they know what to look for and what to expect. Still, the opportunity to review an event multiple times usually enables even more to be seen and remembered. Because learners, like novice sports fans and chess players, typically perceive less than experts do when observing clinical events and because learners are also likely to remember less, they can benefit greatly from having multiple opportunities to observe events that they are to critique.

Video enables peers to do detailed reviews of their work.

As we've discussed in previous chapters, video recordings of clinical events enable viewers to do in-depth reviews that are difficult or impossible to do otherwise. Peers can replay the same 40-second segment of a procedure as many times as they want or need to. They can review it in slow motion, frame by frame, with and without sound.

Video enables learners to experience patients and challenges they might otherwise not have.

By watching video recordings of their peers with patients, learners can broaden their experiences and meet a wider array of patients than they would otherwise. Every patient offers learners opportunities to learn more about such matters as the etiologies of illness, the variety of ways that illness can present in different people, and the impact of illness and treatment on people and their behavior. Irby (1986) contended that the weakest link in experiential clinical learning is in "generalizing from the particular experiences to a general principle applicable in other circumstances" (p. 36). By observing patients on video recordings and discussing them during the course of peer reviews, learners can try to identify general principles they can use in their care of people.

In addition, learners can experience patients in ways not available in real life. For example, in an attempt to better understand patients and their conditions, while viewing a video, they can focus steadily and directly on the patient and the patient's body (in motion and in freeze-frame) in ways that would be socially uncomfortable, unacceptable, or impossible if they were watching that clinical encounter in real life.

Video can enable peers to explore various ways of handling challenges.

There is often more than one way to interact effectively with patients and to handle various challenges that occur. Learners can build their repertoires of responses by sharing strategies with each other. For example, when reviewing the recording of a learner's interaction with a patient, you (or the learner) can stop the tape at decision points, explore what the learner did at that juncture, and then invite peers to suggest and discuss other approaches. Or you can videotape several learners as each of them interacts with the same simulated patient who initially presents in the same way with each of them. You can then replay the interviews, comparing and contrasting the approaches used by the different learners.

ISSUES AND CONSIDERATIONS

Self-critique needs to be part of most peer review processes.

Peer review sessions, like regular supervisory teaching, tend to proceed best when they begin with the designated learner (the person who is the focus of the session) offering his or her self-critique. The arguments for beginning with self-critique in peer review sessions are the same as for other instructional events (see Chapter 6).

If peers are to be helpful to the designated learner, they need to know where he is starting from and what he sees as his needs. The best way to get this information is to ask the learner for his self-assessment before comments are made by others. In addition, all of the learners in the group are likely to be far more comfortable taking their turns as the subjects of a review session if they know they will have the opportunity to identify their areas of need before these are pointed out by others.

Using a video recording as the basis of peer reviews can be unnerving to some learners.

When a learner's oral presentation or her notes in the patient chart are the basis of a peer review session, her peers can have only a vague sense of the real event. They are limited to the information that the learner provides. They do not get to witness whatever awkward or discomforting events may have occurred. Video recordings, however, capture the actual event in living color, which makes it both instructionally more powerful and potentially discomforting. If learners are uneasy about something they said or did while being recorded, understandably, they may not want their peers to view that recording.

Peer review needs to take place in an atmosphere of trust.

As just noted, being asked to be candid when reviewing and critiquing one's performance in the presence of peers can be unsettling, especially in competitive environments in which learners fear that any deficiencies they reveal may be used against them. For the others in the group, being expected to provide feedback to a peer also involves taking risks. Even if a peer tries to give feedback to the designated learner in caring ways, the learner may not be able to separate the message from the messenger and may become defensive, even angry. With this in mind, it's not surprising that some peers withhold their feedback even when they intend it to be helpful.

When learners are expected to critique each other and talk about personal issues, it is essential to take the time needed for building trust and a spirit of collaboration among them. Learners should not be asked to take risks in situations where trust could be broken, where one of the other learners could use what they have seen or heard to cause embarrassment or pain. In general, the more risks that learners are expected to take, the more time needs to be allowed for building relationships among peers. If we pressure learners to take significant risks when they are in the presence of peers they do not trust, we can destroy whatever trust we have managed to build in our own relationships with these learners, and the learning experience will be far less valuable than it might have been. Shortly, we provide some suggestions for steps to take in building trust.

Peer review needs to occur in a collaborative rather than competitive context.

In too many educational settings, learners are pitted against each other. Because of strategies such as grading on a curve, students are forced to compete against each other for a limited number of high grades. In such environments, when one learner helps another learner, she risks helping her peer raise his grade at the expense of her grade. In these settings, peer review can be a high-risk activity for learners and is unlikely to go well.

In educational settings in which collaborative relationships are fostered, learners are rewarded, not penalized, for helping each other. Learners view helping each other as an expectation, as a natural, essential part of the educational process.

Peer review is likely to be most effective if it is a regular part of the educational program.

In general, peer review is most successful when it is done routinely, rather than episodically. Building trust and fostering collaboration among learners takes time, particularly if you and your learners are part of a school or program that is dominated by an authoritarian approach to teaching and learning or if your learners came to you from such programs. Helping learners develop the skills needed for effective peer review also takes time. As the learners' discomfort diminishes and their skills increase, peer review can become increasingly valuable. And if you've done your job, your presence is less and less necessary. Eventually, your learners can conduct most or all of the sessions by themselves.

SUGGESTIONS

PREPARING LEARNERS FOR PEER REVIEW

When preparing learners for peer review, a crucial, overriding task is creating a climate of trust between and among them and you. Many of the steps we recommend below and summarize in the checklist at the end of the chapter (Appendix 8.3) relate to this central task.

In earlier chapters, we described the following tasks which pertain to all review sessions:

- Review the recording as close to the taped event as possible.
- Be sure that you and the learners have privacy.
- Teach learners how to use the video equipment if they don't already know how to.

- **Elicit the learners' views about the value of feedback in learning.**

If learners do not appear to understand the value of feedback and the circumstances lend themselves to some lightness, consider asking the group to participate in an exercise that helps to dramatize the importance of feedback. For example, blindfold one member of the group, give him a ball, place a wastebasket somewhere in the room (but don't tell him where), and then ask him to throw the ball into the wastebasket. Initially, do not give him feedback. Once he and the others acknowledge how impossible the task is without feedback, invite group members to give him feedback that is intended to guide his efforts (e.g., You threw the ball about one foot to the left of the wastebasket).

If you have enough students and want to demonstrate the value of both feedback and collaboration, consider dividing the group in half. Do the same kind of exercise, but have the members of Group 1 give their peer only general feedback (e.g., "good," "bad," "going in the right direction") while inviting members of Group 2 to give their peer very specific feedback (e.g., "You were 2 feet to the left and 3 feet short"). After completing the exercises, discuss some of the issues that surfaced.

- **Discuss the learners' experiences with critiquing their performance in the presence of peers, particularly when using a video recording.**

Find out how many of the group members have critiqued their performance in front of peers. (Their experiences could have been in school, while learning a sport, or in another setting.) Some of them may have never had such an experience. Ask those who have done peer review to describe both the positives and negatives of their experiences. Don't push students to talk about experiences they are not ready to discuss publicly. Try using their experiences as springboards for discussions about the potential value of self-assessment and video review.

- **Discuss the learners' experiences with receiving feedback from peers.**

Ask learners to describe both their positive and negative experiences and to try identifying what caused such experiences to be good or bad. In most groups, you will find at least one person who describes a positive experience that can serve as an opportunity for clarifying the sort of environment you want to create.

- **Explore the learners' experiences with giving feedback to others, particularly peers during peer reviews based on video recordings.**

Ask learners to talk about the circumstances under which they have given feedback to peers. Explore particularly what they felt comfortable doing and what made them feel uncomfortable. Again, expand on their observations to emphasize the rationale for your instructional plans.

- **Discuss the rationale for having peers provide feedback to each other.**

Some of the reasons for having peers provide feedback were discussed above.

- As professionals, learners need to review each other's work.
- Learners can teach each other.
- Being reflective about their peers' work can help learners be more reflective about their own work.
- The task of coaching others fosters critical-mindedness about one's own priorities in learning that may not otherwise be considered.

- **Review the principles of effective feedback.**

You might begin by asking the learners to generate their own list of principles or guidelines. Then add others they have not included. Principles alone tend to be too abstract; they are unlikely to lead to consistent behavior. As you review these principles, cite specific examples of the principles in action. Invite the learners to do the same. Consider using the "Self-Checklist: Giving Feedback to Peers" in Appendix 8.1 as an outline for your discussion. You will note the parallels to "Self-Checklist: Giving Feedback to Learners," Appendix 7.1.

- **If learners are using evaluation forms, make sure they understand all of the items and how to use the forms.**

Because statements on evaluation forms need to be brief, they are often insufficiently communicative. If that is the case with evaluation forms the learners are to use, take time to go over each item, citing specific examples.

Consider having peers use a form that parallels a form that will be completed by the designated learner. The form could also parallel the form you will use if you are participating in the group. For example, see Appendix 6.3 for a sample form that a student could use to assess how she opens an interview. See Appendix 8.2 for a parallel form the student's peers could use to assess how the designated learner opens the interview, and see Appendix 7.2 for a form for teachers to use.

As when using parallel evaluation forms for one-on-one supervision, parallel evaluation forms used for peer review can help focus the review and provide opportunities for designated learners to compare their self-assessments with assessments of their work by others (in this case both their supervisor and peers). When using these forms for peer review, peers can also compare how their assessments of their colleague compare with assessments provided by others. If you have succeeded in establishing an atmosphere of trust and collaboration, these comparisons can be highly instructive.

- **Discuss the format for the review session, including the learners' roles and your role.**

A format to consider:

- Give the remote control to the designated learner (i.e., the learner whose recording is being critiqued).
- Invite designated learners to stop the tape frequently to reflect on the issues they want to explore.
- Invite designated learners to stop the tape whenever they recognize a decision point.
- Invite peers to signal the designated learner whenever they want him or her to stop the tape.
- Tell designated learners that you also will signal them to stop the tape when you have something to say.

- If you have established specific goals for the sessions, encourage everyone to give their primary attention to issues that link to those goals.

- **Establish ground rules for providing critique.**

To minimize the risk that the feedback offered by peers might be distracting or harmful, establish ground rules in advance. Most peers do not want to hurt each other. Yet there is always a risk that some learners will be challenging or demeaning in nonconstructive ways, particularly in those institutions where the grading system and other aspects of the environment promote competition or where some of their teachers/role models use a demeaning style of providing feedback. You might want to use some or all of the items in the checklist in Appendix 8.1 ("Self-Checklist: Giving Feedback to Peers") as ground rules. Following are ground rules for you and the learners to consider:

- Protect the patient's anonymity, both inside the group and in any conversations that occur with others outside the group.
- Do not discuss any personal information about peers that is revealed during the review with anyone outside the group.
- Don't put down or humiliate each other.
- Honor requests from group members to keep certain information private or confidential.

If the group will be meeting multiple times for peer review, the ground rules can be revised as appropriate.

FACILITATING PEER REVIEW, USING VIDEO

Ultimately, you may want groups of learners to conduct some or all of the peer review sessions by themselves. If, however, your learners are not yet ready to do this, there are a number of steps you can take to prepare them.

- **Invite the designated learner to review his or her goals for the event that was taped.**

To be helpful to the learner, you and the group need to know what the learner was trying to accomplish during the interview, exam, procedure, or other event that was taped.

- **Invite the learner to identify any particular help he or she would like from you and the group.**

To provide high-quality care, health professionals need to be able to seek consultation from colleagues. This includes seeking feedback from trusted peers on issues involving their performance. Inviting learners to ask for particular assistance during a critique session gives them an opportunity to practice seeking advice and feedback. For example, in response to your invitation a student might begin her review by saying, "I was trying to appear nonjudgmental because I have a tendency to prejudge patients like this man who abuses alcohol. See what you think." Or "As you'll see, my patient got very angry with me. I don't know what I did wrong. I'd appreciate your thoughts."

- **If appropriate, propose additional goals and issues for the review session.**

As in one-on-one supervision, you might have some goals or issues that you would like to add to the agenda for the review session.

- **If necessary, negotiate and prioritize the learning goals.**

If there is limited time, you and the designated learner might need to prioritize the items on the agenda for the review session. Consider holding a subsequent session if there are more high-priority issues than can be properly managed in the available time.

- **If the peers did not witness the live event, consider playing the event all the way through once before returning for a detailed review.**

Particularly if the learners are relatively new to the skills being critiqued or to the process of peer review, it can be helpful for them to review part or all of the video recording prior to the more detailed review. (If they will be focusing only on part of the taped encounter, say, the closing of the interview, consider playing only that section, unless that segment needs to be seen within the context of the entire interview.)

- **While learners are witnessing the initial playback, encourage them to take notes or fill out the evaluation forms.**

Taking notes while they are witnessing the live or taped event helps learners remember issues and details they might otherwise forget. It also gives them a record of their insights that they can then compare with the ideas and issues that emerge during the subsequent review.

- **When you interact with the designated learner, model the ways you want the learners to help each other.**

Our actions speak louder than our words. Especially during the first peer review sessions, model the various behaviors you want your learners to emulate. For example, if you want the peers to acknowledge when their feedback is subjective, use "I" language when presenting your subjective feedback: "I suspect you were getting angry with Mr. Jones." If necessary, draw attention to the strategies and approaches you are modeling.

- **Make sure that the review process includes a balanced, constructive discussion of the learner's work.**

Most recordings of learners' work include interactions that have effective as well as suboptimal components. If the review session appears to be unbalanced in one direction or another, try to bring about some balance. For example, if the peers are trying to be supportive by focusing only on what the learner did well but appear to be avoiding or ignoring an area in which the learner needs help, consider modeling a way of discussing the learner's problem area in a constructive, supportive way.

- **Help learners extract general principles and strategies that they can use in their future work.**

After discussing how the designated learner handled a particular challenge, as well as other ways the challenge could be handled, invite the learners to try identifying a general principle or strategy that they can draw on when faced with similar situations in the future. If they have difficulty doing this, consider being more directive.

- **If a peer breaks the ground rules, temporarily stop the review process and explore what happened.**

See Chapter 4.

- **Give the learner an opportunity to react to the critiques by his or her peers.**

After a learner receives feedback from her peers, set aside time for this learner to let her peers know what was helpful, what was not helpful, and why. Providing this opportunity regularly will help promote continuing growth in the quality of the feedback that is provided in the group while emphasizing the basic point that learning works best when exchanges move in both directions.

- **Invite the learner to summarize what he or she has learned and identify areas of need.**

Asking a learner to summarize what he learned during the review of his work (including learning needs and goals he identified) can help him pull together and consolidate the issues that emerged during the review session. Making public statements about future learning goals can help learners become more committed to following through on their goals. These summaries can also provide you with diagnostic information about learners' levels of insight and their ability to synthesize and summarize information.

- **Invite the peers to critique their critiques and summarize what they learned.**

When peers critique their critiques, we suggest following the same strategy of first inviting individual learners to critique their critiques and then invite others to offer their feedback. In summarizing what they have learned, learners can include what they have learned about health care as well as what they have learned about themselves and the peer review process.

- **Provide the learners with your assessment of their self-critiques and their critiques of others.**

If learners are to enhance their ability to assess their own performance and provide feedback to each other, they need constructive critique on the approaches they use. Providing feedback to your learners about their process of giving feedback to each other can sharpen your feedback skills while also offering the learners a role model of approaches they can use when providing feedback.

- **If peer review will be ongoing, gradually turn leadership of the group over to the learners.**

Being an effective teacher is analogous in many ways to being an effective parent. In the role of facilitator, we help our students or children develop capabilities that enable them to move forward with less and less supervision until they are able to function successfully without us. To do this, we need to define our success in terms of what we are able to help learners do for themselves rather than in terms of what we do to and for them.

Appendix 8.1

Self-Checklist for Peers: Giving Feedback to Peers

Did I . . .

- ☐ Find out what my colleague was trying to accomplish in the taped encounter?
- ☐ Find out if there were any special issues my colleague wanted me and his or her other peers to focus on in the review session?
- ☐ Invite my colleague's self-assessment before providing my feedback?
- ☐ Try to facilitate my colleague's own discoveries wherever possible?
- ☐ Regard the review as a time to be helpful to my colleague, not to display my insights and expertise?
- ☐ Try to keep the provision of high-quality health care as an overriding concern?
- ☐ Check out my hypotheses about my colleague's behaviors before making pronouncements?
- ☐ Before giving feedback, think through how I would feel receiving these comments?
- ☐ Present feedback in nonjudgmental language?
- ☐ Try to be as specific as possible, referring my colleague to events in the tape when possible?
- ☐ Focus on my colleague's behavior, rather than making judgments about him or her as a person?
- ☐ When my feedback was subjective, label it as such?
- ☐ Provide feedback on my colleague's strengths and accomplishments as well as on his or her weaknesses and errors?
- ☐ Avoid overloading my colleague with feedback?
- ☐ Demonstrate support for my colleague when providing feedback?
- ☐ Help my colleague turn negative feedback into constructive challenges?
- ☐ Encourage my colleague to invite my feedback and to let me know when it is difficult to hear my feedback?
- ☐ Provide follow-up to my feedback when appropriate?

From: Westberg, J., Jason, H. *Teaching Creatively with Video: Fostering Reflection, Communication and Other Clinical Skills,* New York: Springer Publishing Co., 1994.

Appendix 8.2

Evaluation Form for Peers: Opening of Interview

Key:

Y = Yes   N = No   NA = Not Applicable

Circle the appropriate letters. Use space under items to write specific comments, including examples of what was done effectively and ineffectively. (Use over as needed.)

Did my colleague . . .

Y N NA 1. Greet the patient in a friendly, attentive, respectful manner?

Describe:

Y N NA 2. Attend to introductions?

Describe:

Y N NA 3. Help put the patient at ease (e.g., engage in transitional small talk)?

Describe:

Y N NA 4. Use an open-ended approach (e.g., begin the interview and new topics with open-ended questions)?

Describe:

Y N NA 5. Verbally and nonverbally communicate attentiveness and openness?

Describe:

Y N NA 6. Give the patient an adequate opportunity to identify and discuss his or her reasons for today's visit?

Describe:

Y N NA 7. Find out what the patient hoped to accomplish with this visit (e.g., have questions answered, get a prescription)?

Describe:

Other comments:

From: Westberg, J., Jason, H. *Teaching Creatively with Video: Fostering Reflection, Communication and Other Clinical Skills,* New York: Springer Publishing Co., 1994.

Appendix 8.3

Self-Checklist: Preparing Learners for Peer Review Using Video

Did I . . .

- ☐ Help establish a climate of trust?
- ☐ Ensure that the learners and I had privacy?
- ☐ Teach the learners how to use the video equipment, if they didn't already know how to use it?
- ☐ Elicit the learners' views about the value of self-assessment and feedback in learning?
- ☐ Explore the learners' understandings of and experiences with peer review?
- ☐ Explore the learners' experiences with critiquing their performance in the presence of peers or others?
- ☐ Explore the learners' experiences with receiving feedback?
- ☐ Explore the learners' experiences with giving feedback to others, particularly peers, as part of formal or informal peer review?
- ☐ Invite the learners to discuss the rationale for having peers provide feedback to each other?
- ☐ Review the principles of effective feedback with the learners?
- ☐ Review with the learners any evaluation forms they were expected to use?
- ☐ Discuss the format for the review session, including the learners' roles and my role?
- ☐ Establish ground rules for providing critique?

From: Westberg, J., Jason, H. *Teaching Creatively with Video: Fostering Reflection, Communication and Other Clinical Skills,* New York: Springer Publishing Co., 1994.

Appendix 8.4

Self-Checklist for Educators: Facilitating Peer Review, Using Video

Did I . . .

- ☐ Invite the designated learner to review his or her goals for the taped event?
- ☐ Invite the learner to identify any particular help he or she wanted from the group?
- ☐ Propose additional goals and issues for the review session, if appropriate?
- ☐ Help the learner prioritize his or her goals, especially if time was limited?
- ☐ If the group was new to peer review and the event to be critiqued was not too long, ask the learner to play the entire event once before the detailed review?
- ☐ Encourage the peers to take notes as they watched the recording?
- ☐ Model the way I wanted the peers to help each other?
- ☐ Make sure that the review process included a balanced, constructive discussion of the learner's work?
- ☐ Help learners extract general principles and strategies they can use in their future work?
- ☐ If any peers broke the ground rules, temporarily interrupt the review process and discuss what was happening?
- ☐ Give the learner an opportunity to react to the critiques of his or her peers?
- ☐ Invite the learner to summarize what he or she learned and to identify future learning goals?
- ☐ Invite the peers to critique their critiques and summarize what they learned?
- ☐ Provide the learners with my assessment of their critiques?
- ☐ In general, help prepare learners to take increasing responsibility for the leadership of the review sessions?

From: Westberg, J., Jason, H. *Teaching Creatively with Video: Fostering Reflection, Communication and Other Clinical Skills,* New York: Springer Publishing Co., 1994.

CHAPTER 9

Eliciting Patients' Perspectives

The importance of our attending to patients' perspectives on the care they receive is being increasingly recognized, as can be seen in the growing efforts at health care centers and hospitals to elicit patients' feedback on their care. Typically, this information is gathered by asking patients to complete evaluation forms following a hospital stay or a visit with a provider. The information is then given to the providers, with the goal of helping them enhance their sensitivity and effectiveness.

A growing number of faculty members in health professions schools and programs see the value of ensuring that learners get feedback from patients. Patients and clients are asked to complete questionnaires and evaluation forms following their interactions with learners. Occasionally, real patients or simulated patients are asked to provide live feedback by joining learners and their supervisors in reviewing video recordings of their interactions with the learners. (Typically, patients remain for only part of the review session.) An interesting variation was described by Lewis and colleagues (Lewis, Stokes, Fischetti, & Rutledge, 1988): patients were videotaped during exit interviews. These tapes were then reviewed individually with the residents and others in training who had cared for these patients.

In this chapter, we focus on eliciting the perspectives of patients who are videotaped as they interact with learners. Because simulated patients are increasingly being asked to role play with learners in clinical settings, we also include discussions of some issues related to simulated patients. We

- examine reasons for eliciting patients' perspectives
- explore some issues and considerations to have in mind when working with "real" patients
- provide explicit suggestions for (1) preparing patients for being videotaped and participating in review sessions, (2) preparing learners for review sessions with patients, (3) conducting review sessions, and (4) including peers in the review sessions with the learner and patient.

As is true for the rest of the book, in this chapter the word *client* can usually be substituted for the word *patient*.

REASONS FOR ELICITING PATIENTS' PERSPECTIVES

Patients have unique, important perspectives.

Our learners' patients have unique information. Only they know whether the learners helped them feel at ease, gave them opportunities to talk about their concerns, communicated clearly, touched them gently during exams or procedures, and helped them feel that they were partners in their care. These are subjective matters shaped, in part, by characteristics of the patients, not just the behaviors of the learners. Yet over time, consistency in the observations made by patients can be highly instructive to learners.

When reviewing videotaped patient encounters without patient input, we can only speculate about what the patients were thinking and feeling.

As we study a videotaped encounter with a learner, we can entertain and offer hypotheses about what the patient on the recording was thinking or feeling (e.g., "Mr. J. looks like he has something else he'd like to say" or "It appears that Ms. S. is worried that she has cancer"). If we aren't able to talk with the patient, we can't be certain about the patient's state of mind. However, when patients are present during review sessions, learners can directly ask them what they were thinking and feeling at key points during the interaction.

Patients' feedback can be more powerful than feedback from us.

When we tell learners that we think they were not communicating clearly to their patients, or that they appear judgmental, they can rationalize that we misunderstood what they were doing or that we are being overly critical. However, when a patient says, "I couldn't understand what you were telling me" or "I didn't feel I could talk about my sex life because I wasn't comfortable talking with you about personal matters," students are likely to pay attention. Further, positive feedback directly from patients (e.g., "I could sense how sincerely you wanted to help" or "You really made me feel I could talk to you about anything I wanted") can be high points in their learning experiences.

If learners value patients' feedback, they are likely to seek it when they are in practice.

If learners get helpful feedback from patients during their basic formal education, they are likely to be open to, and even take initiative in seeking, feedback from their patients later. They might, for example, create and use a patient satisfaction questionnaire in their practice, meet with focus groups made up of people from their practice, or both.

WORKING WITH REAL PATIENTS

Patients are unlikely to be candid if they are worried that their feedback will adversely affect the care they receive.

When involving real patients in providing feedback to learners, we need to ensure that their care will not be affected by what they say or do, and we need to communicate this assurance to them. Most people, especially those who have little or no choice about who provides their care and how it is provided, feel vulnerable when seeking and receiving health care. Patients who are only filling out anonymous questionnaires usually feel protected from recrimination. But those who voice their concerns directly to caregivers can be understandably worried that providing feedback, especially negative feedback, might result in suboptimal treatment at subsequent visits.

When selecting patients who will provide face-to-face feedback to learners, there are several characteristics to consider.

Learners can potentially learn important lessons from all patients, but those patients who are most likely to provide learners with helpful feedback typically are somewhat reflective, reasonably articulate, and sufficiently self-confident to not feel intimidated by the task of providing feedback directly to a health professional. For patients to be adequately reflective and articulate also requires that they are not unduly distracted by pain or other symptoms and that they have sufficient energy for the task. Some people who have had multiple experiences with the health care system (e.g., people with chronic conditions) have a rich background to draw on and are able to make helpful comparisons between the learner's performance and the care they have received from other health professionals.

The patient's availability is an important consideration.

The process of videotaping and reviewing an interaction with a learner can increase the length of an encounter, although the amount of extra time needed can be small if thorough preparations have been made in advance. To ensure that ambulatory patients can take time after their visit to participate in a review session usually requires requesting their help and scheduling an extended visit in advance. Working with hospitalized patients or clients in nursing homes or other facilities also requires advance planning so as not to conflict with their care or visitors.

One patient's point of view about a learner's interpersonal skills can be helpful but should not be generalized.

Because patients differ widely in their expectations, needs, and capacity to reflect on and talk about interpersonal matters, one patient's point of view about a learner's skills should not be accorded inflated importance. The patient's feedback may be helpful but must be viewed in perspective. Over time, multiple patients' feedback about a particular learner's skills can begin to provide consistency or form a mosaic that can be especially useful.

There are advantages and disadvantages to working with real patients.

Real patients are instantly credible, so with them you rarely if ever confront the resistance and skepticism expressed by some learners when they are asked to work with simulated patients. In addition, you don't need to train real patients to play a part; they can be themselves. On the other hand, it can take time to find patients who both have the characteristics suggested above and can be reliably available when you need them. Also, you have little or no control over such factors as how real patients present clinically, and how they give feedback to learners. This unpredictability may or may not be desirable, depending on the learning goals. Further, you cannot ask patients who are being cared for by the learner to participate in educational activities that will interfere with their professional relationship with the learner. For example, during the review session it would be inappropriate to press the learner or the learner's actual patient to explore issues that will cause the patient to subsequently question the learner's credibility as a provider. In addition, while real patients are present, care needs to be taken to postpone discussions that might confuse, mislead, or upset them.

SUGGESTIONS

PREPARING PATIENTS FOR BEING VIDEOTAPED AND PARTICIPATING IN REVIEW SESSIONS

Some patients will consent to being videotaped but won't be able to participate in the review process. Consider asking those patients to complete an evaluation form, such as the one in Appendix 9.1. Give the completed form to the learner and include this written patient feedback in your discussion when you and the learner review the video recording.

When orienting patients who will be videotaped and who will provide face-to-face feedback to learners, consider preparing them in three stages. In advance of the videotaped interview, give them a general overview of what is needed. Immediately prior to the taping, review what will happen during the taping. Immediately prior to the review session, talk with both the patient and learner about what will happen in the review session.

Following are suggestions for steps to take when preparing real patients for being videotaped and participating in the review process. Most of the steps pertain to topics to cover with a patient who has agreed to talk with you about the possibility of being videotaped and providing critique. Since the patient's agreement to participate needs to be based on an understanding of what will be involved, the overriding goal of the discussion is providing the patient with the information she or he needs for making an informed decision about whether to participate. Later in this chapter we provide specific suggestions for steps to take with the patient and the learner in the review session.

- **Discuss your reasons for inviting patients to provide feedback to health professionals.**

Talk with patients about the reasons that you or your program would appreciate their feedback. Your reasons might include the following:

- Patients have a unique, important perspective.
- Only patients have access to and can provide certain kinds of information.
- Feedback from patients can improve the quality of the care provided.

Let patients know that learners in the health professions need to become and remain as sensitive as possible to the real needs and concerns of patients and that patients are able to provide helpful information that is not available in any other way. For example, only patients know their internal reactions to the approaches used by the learner, such as the extent to which they feel able to be fully candid with the learner and the extent to which they understand explanations and advice provided by the learner.

- **Explain how the videotaping will be done.**

In most cases, patients should be told to be themselves during the taped encounter—to conduct themselves as usual without giving any thought to the review session or, if possible, to the video equipment. Explain where the video camera will be and how it will be operated. If a videographer will be in the room with the learner and patient, explain who this person is, what he or she will be doing, and that the encounter will be held in strict confidence.

- **Explain how the recording will be used.**

If the recording will be used only for the review sessions and the tapes will then be recycled, let patients know this. If the recordings will be used for additional purposes, inform patients about this as well.

- **Explain how the review session will be conducted.**

What you say to the patient about the review session will of course depend on what you plan to do. Prior to the videotaped encounter, it is usually enough to give patients a global sense of what you need from them during the review session. Although you don't want to bog them down with details, you do need to give them enough information so they can decide whether they want to participate.

- **Invite and respond to patients' questions and concerns.**

As we've indicated, a common though often unspoken concern that many people have is that any negative feedback they offer will be used against them when they seek care. Even if patients don't overtly voice this concern, it is important to anticipate it and deal with it, if appropriate.

- **Obtain the patient's informed consent to participate.**

Ensure that patients have all the information they need about the review process and give them the opportunity to decide if they want to participate. Be careful not to exert undue pressure on patients who are reluctant. They should not feel that they must participate to please you or that their refusal to participate will be used against them.

- **Immediately prior to the videotaped encounter, review what will take place, if appropriate.**

If much time has passed since you initially spoke to the patient, review what will happen and invite his or her questions. Focus chiefly on the videotaped encounter, saving a detailed discussion of the review session until immediately before it will take place. If patients become preoccupied with worries about the review session, they may not give their full attention to the videotaped encounter.

PREPARING LEARNERS FOR REVIEW SESSIONS WITH PATIENTS

When preparing learners for review sessions with patients, you can work with one student at a time or with a group of learners. Preparing several learners at one time can save time. And if learners will be working as a group (i.e., taking turns reviewing video recordings with patients in the presence of peers), preparing them together can help them begin functioning as a group.

- **Find out what experiences learners have had with involving patients in review sessions and how these sessions went.**

As always, begin new learning experiences by inquiring about your learners' experiences with whatever you intend to do with them. This information can guide your subsequent steps. For example, if you discover that one of your learners had a strongly negative experience with a simulated patient, you will probably need to address the student's concerns before moving ahead.

- **Discuss the reasons for involving patients in the review process.**

Invite your learners to identify and discuss their views of the reasons for involving simulated or real patients in the review process (e.g., their unique perspectives). Talk about some of the information that patients are uniquely equipped to provide, such as their perceptions of the extent to which the health professional

- encouraged them to explain their concerns fully
- listened carefully to what they said
- used language they could understand

- clearly explained the reasons for the procedure
- welcomed and responded to their questions
- was as gentle as possible when examining them or doing a procedure.

- **Give learners specific suggestions for eliciting feedback from patients.**

Let your students know that patients are most likely to be candid if they (the learners) let patients know that their input is valued and that their feedback is sincerely solicited (if such is indeed the case). For example, when learners are going to engage in a review session with a simulated patient, you might suggest that the learners say something like "I hope as we review this recording of our interview that you'll be as candid as possible in pointing out things I did that bothered you as well as things I did that you thought were helpful."

Let learners know that this is a unique opportunity to find out what patients are thinking and feeling during critical parts of the encounter, with questions such as "How did you feel when I confronted you about your smoking?"

Review sessions with patients are also a time to find out about concerns and issues learners didn't raise during the encounter: "Was there anything you had wanted to talk about but didn't?"

CONDUCTING REVIEW SESSIONS

Here we focus on review sessions that include a teacher, a learner, and a patient. Next we'll provide suggestions for including the learner's peers in the review session.

- **Create a climate of trust.**

Work to create a friendly, supportive, nonconfrontational atmosphere. (Many of the following steps are intended to create this atmosphere.) Let the learner and patient know that you aren't putting them under pressure to come up with anything in particular and that the session can be very brief if there is only a little to discuss. (Typically there is a great deal to discuss.)

- **Be sure that you, the learner, and the patient have privacy.**

Treat the review session with the same concern for privacy that you treat any clinical encounter.

- **If the learner and/or patient are using evaluation forms, be sure they understand the items and how to fill them out.**

Evaluation forms designed for patients to use in evaluating their provider, such as the one in Appendix 9.1, can help patients provide reactions on those issues that they are particularly well equipped to discuss. A parallel form for the provider (Appendix 9.2) enables learners to compare their independently recorded self-critiques with the evaluations provided by their patients. It can be very useful to compare the patient's reasons for the encounter (i.e., the reasons he or she sought help at this time) with the provider's perception of the patient's reasons for the encounter. Providers don't always pick up on their patients' real reasons for encounters. Also, it can be useful for the learner and patient to compare their separate understandings of the management plan or the plans for other actions.

Generally, it is best to have the learner and provider fill out their evaluation forms before beginning the critique process, so that they are not influenced by the subsequent discussions of the video recording.

The learner and patient can discuss what they've written on their evaluation forms before proceeding with the critique of the video recording or later in the session. Some of the factors to consider when deciding when and how to give the learner the patient's written feedback include the learner's comfort with the review process, the patient's comfort with the process, whether you feel the written comments will facilitate or block the review process, and the amount of time you have.

- **Review the format for the critique session, including the patient's role, the learner's role, and your role.**

Briefly review the format. The suggestions that follow imply a particular format that you may or may not want to adopt. Include guidelines about who will pause the tape and how this will be done. For example, you can give the remote control to the learner, or all of you can sit close enough to the playback machine so that any of you can reach over and pause the playback whenever you choose.

- **Consider asking the patient to summarize his or her reactions to the encounter with the learner.**

It can be useful to gather information from the patient before the patient's thoughts and feelings have been influenced by what you and the learner say. Be careful, however, not to make patients feel that they must provide a critique if they are not yet ready to do so.

- **Invite the learner to identify his or her goals for the review session.**

Some teachers include the patient in only the first part of the review session. Then they excuse the patient, and the session continues with a discussion of issues that would not be of interest to the patient or issues that can't or shouldn't be discussed in the patient's presence (e.g., some of the learner's personal issues, speculations that the learner has about the patient's problems that he first wants to discuss with his supervisor). If the patient will be present for only part of the review session, ask the learner to identify what he or she would like to address and accomplish while the patient is present.

- **If appropriate, propose additional goals and issues for the review session and work with the learner in prioritizing the goals.**

As we've mentioned in discussing other kinds of review sessions, you may have additional goals and issues that you would like the learner to address during the review session. If there is insufficient time to deal with all of the issues and goals that you and the learner propose, work with the learner in prioritizing the goals, perhaps saving some of them for review and discussion at another time.

- **If necessary, initiate the process of stopping the tape.**

If, initially, the learner and patient appear to be uncomfortable stopping the tape (as is common), consider stopping it yourself and inviting them to comment on the thoughts or feelings they were having at that point in the encounter.

- **Be sure the patient understands the importance of identifying both the positive and negative aspects of the encounter.**

Before beginning the critique session, consider reiterating the importance for all three of you to identify and discuss both the positive and negative aspects of the encounter. If during the review session the critique tends to be unbalanced, take steps to introduce balance. For example, if most of the critique of a student's interview or patient education session has been positive, acknowledge the importance of identifying these positive aspects but note that all interviews or patient education sessions (even those done by experts) can be improved. Encourage the learner and patient to identify ways in which the encounter in question could have been enhanced.

- **If the learner is working with a simulated patient, consider having them role play optional strategies.**

Experts have a variety of strategies available for use in clinical situations. To help learners expand their repertoire of available strategies, consider having them role play optional ways of handling a given situation with the simulated patient. Even encourage them to experiment with some strategies they would not want to attempt for the first time with a real patient (e.g., ways of trying to discover if a patient is being abused by her husband).

- **After the review session, debrief the patient.**

Taking time after the review session to ask the patient the following kinds of questions can provide important information:

- How did you feel about the review session?
- Was there anything you wanted to say that you didn't get to talk about?
- Did any issues come up that have left you with unanswered questions?

Sometimes patients have important insights about the learner that they are reluctant to share during the review session but will share with you when encouraged to do so during the debriefing. Occasionally during debriefing sessions, real or simulated patients will let you know that the encounter and/or review session left them with a personal concern. For example, a real patient might say, "Do you think I should stop taking my medicine? The questions that Mr. Smith asked me made me wonder if my medicine is doing more harm than good." Or after playing the role of a woman with breast cancer, a simulated patient might admit to you, "Actually, I have a lump in my breast that I've been trying to ignore. Do you think I should see my doctor?"

During debriefing sessions, it's important to clear up patients' misunderstandings, but usually these sessions are not appropriate times for providing health care, especially if the person is not your patient. During a debriefing, however, it often is appropriate to acknowledge patients' concerns and be supportive of their seeking further help.

INCLUDING PEERS IN THE REVIEW SESSION WITH THE LEARNER AND PATIENT

There are advantages and disadvantages to including peers in a review session with the learner and patient. The advantages include the following:

- The peers can learn from the patient and from the learner's experience.
- Peers can contribute additional helpful perspectives.
- The collaborative climate you may be trying to build can be reinforced.

Some possible disadvantages of including peers:

- Patients, particularly real patients, might feel overwhelmed by the presence of multiple learners.
- Patients, particularly real patients, might not feel comfortable being totally candid in the presence of people they don't know.

- The learner might not be fully candid in the presence of peers.
- Some peers might want to be the center of attention rather than facilitating the learner's and patient's reflections and dialogue.

- **Create a climate of trust.**

When real or simulated patients are present, take time to be sure that they are comfortable with everyone in the room. This includes asking all members of the group to introduce themselves and to expressly agree that the patient's confidentiality will be protected.

- **If evaluation forms are being used, ensure that everyone understands the items, when and how to fill them out, and how the information will be used.**

There are arguments for using evaluation forms, particularly with a group of learners.

- All learners are challenged to reflect on the encounter, even if they don't speak.
- Evaluation forms can help guide the discussion, if peers will be involved.

In Appendix 9.3 there is an evaluation form for peers to use that parallels the form used by the patient (Appendix 9.1) and the one used by the learner (Appendix 9.2).

- **Review the format for the review session, including everyone's role.**

Above we discussed the roles that you and the learner and patient could play if the three of you were working alone together. Even with peers present, you can still focus on the learner and patient, giving the remote control to the learner as a way of emphasizing his or her central role. Peers can be asked to take a secondary role, asking questions (particularly questions that facilitate the learner's and patient's reflections) and providing feedback that complements and supplements the learner's and patient's work.

- **Invite the learner to take the lead in establishing the goals and agenda for the review, with supplementary input from the patient, you, and, if appropriate, the learner's peers.**

See above for a discussion of setting goals.

- **Be sure the focus stays on the learner and patient.**

In general, review sessions with patients are most fruitful if the focus stays on the learner and patient. However, there are many ways to conduct review sessions, including strategies that more actively include all members of the group.

- **At the end of the review session, consider asking all of the students to summarize what they have learned.**

Be sure that the designated learner's peers make statements about what they have learned, not what they feel the designated learner has learned or should have learned.

Appendix 9.1

Evaluation of Care: Patient's Form

Note: The information that you provide helps us to continually improve the care that we provide. We welcome and appreciate your comments. Thanks!

Provider ______________________________ Date ______________

Reason(s) I came to the health center today

____

____

Using the following key, please indicate the extent to which you agree with each of the statements below by circling the appropriate letter.
A = Always M = Most of the time S = Some of the time
N = Never U = I am Unable to evaluate this at this time.

During this visit, the provider . . .

1. A M S N U gave me a chance to explain why I came for care today.
2. A M S N U listened carefully to what I said.
3. A M S N U used words that I could easily understand.
4. A M S N U encouraged me to ask questions.
5. A M S N U helped me work out a plan to take care of myself (or my family member).
6. A M S N U treated me with dignity and respect.
7. A M S N U wanted me to be a partner in taking care of my health.

What did you like about this visit?

____

How could this visit have been improved?

____

Please summarize your understanding of the plan that you and the provider agreed upon (e.g., further tests, medications you need to take).

____

____

____

From: Westberg, J., Jason, H. *Teaching Creatively with Video: Fostering Reflection, Communication and Other Clinical Skills,* New York: Springer Publishing Co., 1994.

Appendix 9.2

Evaluation of Care: Provider's Form

Provider ______________________________ Date ________________

Patient's name ____

Patient's stated reasons for encounter.

____

____

Using the following key, please indicate the extent to which you agree with each of the statements below by circling the appropriate letter.
A = Always M = Most of the time S = Some of the time
N = Never U = I am Unable to evaluate this at this time.

During the visit, I . . .

1. A M S N U gave the patient a chance to explain why he or she came for care (reasons for encounter).
2. A M S N U listened carefully to what the patient said.
3. A M S N U used language that the patient could easily understand.
4. A M S N U encouraged the patient to ask questions.
5. A M S N U worked with the patient in developing a management plan.
6. A M S N U treated the patient with dignity and respect.
7. A M S N U conveyed the message that I wanted the patient to be a partner in taking care of his or her health.

Summarize the plan that you and the patient agreed upon (e.g., further tests, medications).

____

____

____

____

____

____

From: Westberg, J., Jason, H. *Teaching Creatively with Video: Fostering Reflection, Communication and Other Clinical Skills,* New York: Springer Publishing Co., 1994.

Appendix 9.3

Evaluation of Care:
Peer's Form

Peer ______________________ Date ____________

Provider ______________ Patient ______________

Patient's stated reasons for encounter.

____

____

Using the following key, please indicate the extent to which you agree with each of the statements below by circling the appropriate letter.
A = Always M = Most of the time S = Some of the time
N = Never U = I am Unable to evaluate this at this time.

During this visit, the provider . . .

1. A M S N U gave the patient a chance to explain why he or she came for care (reasons for encounter).
2. A M S N U listened carefully to what the patient said.
3. A M S N U used language that the patient could easily understand.
4. A M S N U encouraged the patient to ask questions.
5. A M S N U worked with the patient in developing a management plan.
6. A M S N U treated the patient with dignity and respect.
7. A M S N U conveyed the message that he/she wanted the patient to be a partner in taking care of his or her health.

Summarize the plan that the provider and the patient agreed upon (e.g., further tests, medications).

____

____

____

____

____

____

From: Westberg, J., Jason, H. *Teaching Creatively with Video: Fostering Reflection, Communication and Other Clinical Skills,* New York: Springer Publishing Co., 1994.

Appendix 9.4

Self-Checklist for Educators: Reviewing Video Recordings with Learners and Patients

Did I . . .

- ☐ Create a climate of trust?
- ☐ Make sure that the learner, the patient, and I had privacy?
- ☐ Make sure that the learner and patient understood the items on any evaluation forms they needed to fill out and how to complete the forms?
- ☐ Review the format for the critique session, including the patient's role, the learner's role, and my role?
- ☐ Give primary control over the playback process to the learner?
- ☐ Invite the learner to identify his or her goals for the review session?
- ☐ Invite the patient to share any issues he or she hoped would be addressed?
- ☐ Propose additional goals and issues, if appropriate?
- ☐ Negotiate and help the learner prioritize the goals, if necessary?
- ☐ Initiate the process of stopping the tape, if necessary?
- ☐ Make sure the patient understood the importance of identifying both the positive and negative aspects of the encounter?
- ☐ If the learner was working with a simulated patient, have him or her and the patient role play optional strategies?
- ☐ Debrief the patient after the review session?

Comments:

From: Westberg, J., Jason, H. *Teaching Creatively with Video: Fostering Reflection, Communication and Other Clinical Skills,* New York: Springer Publishing Co., 1994.

Epilogue

If you've read through—or at least skimmed through—this book, you may be among those who conclude that there is more to using video in teaching than you had anticipated or, perhaps, even wanted to know. You may also be wondering: is all that attention to technical detail and all that concern about trust and emphasizing the learners' self-assessments really so important? The short answer is: no, not unless you want to be more than a transient or negative event in your learners' lives.

If you are serious about trying to make a worthy, sustained difference, if you are intent on leaving your learners better equipped for their professional tasks, not just able to pass some current exams, then the challenges you face are considerable. Many of our learners come to us from instructional experiences that cause them to be less than optimal learners. Most of them feel pressured and distracted; many of them have come to see themselves as along for the ride, not as being in the driver's seat. Some feel like victims. In brief, too many of our learners are less than fully ready to learn.

To break through their sense of being overloaded and their adopted posture of passivity and dependence, we need access to powerful techniques and tools. As we have tried to explain throughout this book, we see video as having more potential as the right tool for the job than anything else currently available or on the horizon. But, like other tools, video can only be as effective as those who use it. And, also like other tools, it has the potential for harm as well as help.

So, inescapably, as is so disappointingly often the case, there is no free lunch. We must do far more than purchase the right equipment and switch it on. Ultimately, we are back to an ancient truism: the key to good teaching is the teacher. Even with the help of video, our preparation, skills, commitments, and level of effort are vital elements in assuring that students achieve learning that is worthy and enduring.

Few of us have had sufficient preparation for either the psychological or the technical demands of skilled teaching. Equally few are in programs where high-quality teaching is sought and rewarded. And, as we've pointed out, there is no easy, technological quick-fix. So, what is an aspiring teacher to do?

As the Chinese aphorism reminds us, "Even a journey of a thousand miles begins with a single step." Our effort in this book has been to offer you a considerable assortment of possible steps to take on the never-ending journey of refining our instructional skills and enhancing the contributions we make to our learners. Perhaps the most important step is acknowledging the complexity of the task and remaining committed, even optimistic, nonetheless. The rest is details: overcoming our tendency to jump in with feedback prematurely, encouraging learners to think about their goals, enhancing the clarity of our explanations with well-selected video triggers.

There are at least three components to the process of mastering the use of video. We hope this book has given you a start with two of them: understanding what is needed for handling the technical side of using video and, more importantly, knowing what is involved in managing the human aspects of incorporating video into your teaching. A book, however, is incapable of giving you the third element: the determination needed for becoming skillful in applying the first two components and for creating the context in which video can fulfill its potential for your learners. Our largest hope is that you will bring this determination to your teaching.

We also hope—in fact, wish—for you that you are having or will soon have the full measure of joy and fulfillment that can accompany the process of teaching when you and your learners realize that you are doing everything you can to respond to what they really need for becoming highly competent professionals. We wish you every success in achieving and maintaining such experiences . . . for yourself and your learners.

Glossary

Address A specific location in a television recording as specified by the *time code*.

Audio The sound portion of television and its production, including spoken words, music, and ambient sound. Technically, the electronic reproduction of audible sound.

Audio mixer An electronic device that enables the mixing of two or more independent audio sources that might each require separate levels of amplification.

Backlight Illumination from behind the subject, facing the camera.

Black Blank videotape shows up on a television screen as "snow" or "noise." A *black burst generator* can be used to create a pure black image on the videotape. A lower-quality black can be created by running a television camera with its lens cap on while in the record mode.

Black burst generator An electronic device that puts out a signal that registers as pure black when recorded on videotape.

Breakup The loss of a clear, steady video image.

Bump-up Copy (dub) a tape to a higher-level *format*.

Bust shot A shot of a person beginning just above the bust line.

Camcorder Single unit, incorporating both video camera and video recorder.

Character generator A device that electronically produces a series of letters and numbers, enabling text to be overlaid on a television image at the time of presentation or incorporated into the image at the time of editing.

Close-up A shot that fills the screen with the subject or with only a portion of the subject. The close-up (CU) can range from an extreme close-up (ECU)—made popular by the television program *60 Minutes*—to relatively loose, as in a medium close-up (MCU).

Depth of field The area in which all objects, located at different distances from the camera, appear in focus. Depth of field is dependent upon focal length of the lens, f-stop (size of opening of the lens), and distance between object and camera. Directors vary the depth of field of shots, from shallow to deep, to achieve desired effects.

Dissolve A gradual transition between shots in which the two images temporarily overlap.

Dropout A loss of picture or part of the picture, usually caused by imperfections on a videotape. Dropout typically is seen as tiny white or silver flecks on the video screen.

Dub The duplication of a video recording. The dub is always one generation away from the recording used for making it.

Dubbing down Also referred to as bumping down. The dubbing (transfer) of picture and sound information from a higher-quality quality *format* to a lower one. (Same as *bumping-up*).

Dubbing up Also referred to as bumping up. The dubbing (transfer) of picture and sound information from a lower *format* videotape to a higher one.

Editing The selection and assembly of shots into a particular sequence.

Establishing shot Usually a *long shot* that gives viewers an overview and context of the scene.

Fixed camera A camera that is permanently installed or remains in the same place during a shoot.

Format Type of recording medium (usually, the type of videotape used when making video recordings). Consumer (lower-level) formats include VHS and 8mm. Eeducational/industrial formats include S-VHS and 3/4-inch U-matic. Professional formats are Betacam and MII.

Framing Similar to a picture frame, the outer borders of the image captured through the camera's lens.

Freeze frame Arrested motion that is perceived as a still shot.

Generation The number of dubs away from the original tape. The first generation is the camera master. The second generation is usually the edited master. A dub made directly from the edited tape would be a third generation, and so on. The greater the number of nondigital generations, the greater the quality loss.

High-angle shot A shot taken with a camera placed high, looking down at the subject. High angles tend to diminish the viewer's sense of the subject.

In-cue Time code or other information indicating the beginning of a segment on the tape you want to use (e.g., for editing or teaching). Also referred to as "in-point."

In-point See *In-cue*.

Index, Indexing The capability of some cameras and videocassette recorders (VCRs) to insert an electronic signal at selected points on a tape, enabling those points to be found rapidly on playback.

Insert mode, Insert editing A mode of editing in which a segment is inserted into an already existing recording, overwriting whatever currently exists on the tape that is the length of the inserted segment.

Knee shot A shot of a person beginning just above the knee.

Lavaliere An extremely small microphone that can be clipped onto a jacket, blouse, or other piece of clothing. A slightly larger model is suspended from a neck cord and worn in the front of the chest.

Long shot Sometimes called a *wide shot*. The object is seen from far away or framed very loosely. The extreme long shot (ELS) shows the object from a great distance.

Loose When some directors want the camera operator to expand the field of vision, they will ask the operator to "loosen" the shot.

Low-angle shot A shot taken from a low camera position looking up at the subject. This shot tends to make the subject appear more dominant to the viewer.

Medium shot Object seen from a medium distance.

Out-cue *Time code* or other information indicating the end of the segment of video you want to use (e.g., for editing or teaching).

Over-the-shoulder shot Camera looks at a person (often in an interview) from a perspective showing another person's (the interviewer's) shoulder and part of the back of his/her head.

Pan Horizontal movement of the camera.

Playback The playing back on a monitor, projection screen, or television receiver of recorded videotape.

Point of view A way of describing what the camera sees as thought of in terms of a person who would be at the camera's vantage point. For example, a child's point of view implies that the camera is looking up from a relatively low position.

Remote A television production done outside the studio.

Rewritable consumer code (RC) Time code developed for the consumer market by Sony Corporation, providing frame-accurate address information. (See *SMPTE time code*.)

Running time The duration of a program, also called program length.

Shoot A session of video recording.

Shot The single, continuous take of material recorded from the time the camera and recorder are turned on until they are paused or turned off.

SMPTE time code An electronic signal recorded on the cue or address track of videotape or on an audio track of multitrack audiotape using a time-code generator, providing a time address for each frame in hours, minutes, seconds, and frame numbers of elapsed tape. There are 30 frames per second. Developed by the Society of Motion Picture and Television Engineers.

Static shot A shot that does not change.

Steadicam jr A small hand-held device to which camcorders can be attached, enabling a person with sufficient practice to move the camera in almost any direction while maintaining a smooth, steady image on the screen.

Three-shot A shot that includes three people.

Tight When some directors want the camera operator to reduce the field of vision, they will ask the operator to "tighten" the shot.

Tilting Pointing the camera up or down.

Time code An electronic frame-numbering system based on the 24-hour clock that assigns every frame of videotape (there are 30 frames per second) a unique number. Typically, the number indicates the elapsed number of hours, minutes, seconds, and frames from the start of the recording. (See *SMPTE time code* and *Rewritable Consumer code.)*

Tripod A three-legged camera mount, often standing on a wheeled dolly for easy maneuverability.

Two-shot A shot that includes two people.

VCR See *videocassette recorder*.

VHS See *Video Home System*.

Videocassette Similar in construction to an audiocasette. A plastic container in which a videotape moves between a supply reel and a take-up reel. The tape is played through a videocassette recorder.

Videocassette recorder (VCR) A recording and playback device that records and stores on videotape video and audio signals for later playback or postproduction editing.

Video clips Brief segments of longer video programs.

Videographer Camera operator.

Video Home System (VHS) A half-inch video format that dominates the home market.

Video log A term we use for tape(s) that contain two or more segments (e.g., of learners interacting with patients) shot over time so that learners have a historical record of their progress, or lack of progress.

Video-triggers Brief (often less than two minutes long), usually incomplete events (vignettes) that are used for stimulating discussion, provoking intellectual and emotional reactions, and giving learners practice in dealing with challenges.

Viewfinder The eyepiece through which you see the framing of the image as the camera sees it and as it will be recorded on the videotape. In virtually all modern video cameras, when you look through the eyepiece of the viewfinder, you are actually seeing through the lens through which the video recording will be made.

Visual scanning A capacity of a video playback machine that enables you to see the picture fairly clearly while you fast-forward or rapidly rewind the tape.

Wide-angle lens A lens that provides a large field of vision, typically larger than the field of vision of the human eye if the head is kept in a fixed position. When using a wide-angle lens, objects relatively close to the camera look large and objects only a short distance away look small.

Window-burn A dub of a tape, usually of the source tapes for an edit, onto which has been "burned" (superimposed) a small rectangular window that provides a visual display of the running *time code* of the footage being shown.

Zoom in Decrease the field of vision. Tighten the shot.

Zoom lens A lens that has a range of fields of vision, typically from wide to narrow (telephoto).

Zoom out Increase the field of vision. Loosen the shot.

References

Alexander, M., Hall, M. N., & Pettice, Y. J. (1994). Cinemeducation: An innovative approach to teaching psychosocial medical care. *Family Medicine, 26.*

Alfaro, R. (1986). *Applications of nursing process: A step-by-step guide.* Philadelphia: J. B. Lippincott.

Arnold, L., Willoughby, T. L., & Calkins, E. V. (1985). Self-evaluation in undergraduate medical education: A longitudinal perspective. *Journal of Medical Education*, 60: 21–28.

Barrows, H. S. (1985). *How to design a problem-based curriculum for the preclinical years.* New York: Springer Publishing Company.

Barrows, H. S. (1987). *Simulated (standardized) patients and other human simulations.* Chapel Hill, NC: Health Sciences Consortium.

Barrows, H. S., & Tamblyn, P. (1980). *Problem-based learning: An approach to medical education.* New York: Springer Publishing Company.

Brookfield, S. D. (1986). *Understanding and facilitating adult learning.* San Francisco: Jossey-Bass.

Chickering, A. W. (1977). *Experience and learning: An introduction to experiential learning.* New Rochelle, NY: Change Magazine Press.

Cross, K. P. (1986, September). A proposal to improve teaching or what 'taking teaching seriously' should mean. *American Association for Higher Education.* Cited by Garvin, D. A. (1991). Barriers and gateways to learning. In C. R. Christensen, D. A. Garvin, & A. Sweet (Eds.). *Education for judgment: The artistry of discussion leadership.* (pp. 3–13). Boston: Harvard Business School Press.

De Groot, A. D. (1946). *Het denken van den Schaker* [*Thinking processes in chess players*]. Den Haag, The Netherlands: Noord Holland.

Dowrick, P. W., & Jesdale, D. C. (1991). Modeling. In Dowrick, P. W. (Ed.), *Practical guide to using video in the behavioral sciences.* (pp. 64–76). New York: John Wiley & Sons.

Educational film/video locator of the consortium of university film centers and R. R. Bowker. (1990). 4th ed. New York: R. R. Bowker.

Elstein, A. S., Shulman, L. S., & Sprafka, S. A. (1978). *Medical problem solving: An analysis of clinical reasoning*. Cambridge, MA: Harvard University Press.

Ende, J. (1983). Feedback in clinical medical education. *Journal of the American Medical Association,* 250(6): 777–781.

Feidel, D., & Bolm G. (1981). Self-confrontation through video-playback in courses of medical psychology: A summary evaluation of Kagan's Interpersonal Process Recall method in a German adaptation. *Medizinische Psychologie* 7: 71–72.

Finley, B., Kim, K., & Mynatt, S. (1979). Maximizing videotaped learning of interpersonal skills. *Journal of Nursing Education,* 18: 33–41.

Franks, I. M., & Maile, L. J. (1991). The use of video in sport skill acquisition. In P. W. Dowrick, (Ed.), *Practical guide to using video in the behavioral sciences* (pp. 231–243). New York: John Wiley & Sons.

Fuller, F., & Manning, B. A. (1973, Fall). Self-confrontation reviewed: A conceptualization for video playback in teacher education. *Review of Educational Research,* 469–528.

Gagne, R. M. (1965). *The conditions of learning.* New York: Holt, Rinehart and Winston.

Hall, E. G., & Erffmeyer, E. S. (1983). The effect of visuomotor behavior rehearsal with videotaped modeling on free throw accuracy of intercollegiate female basketball players. *Journal of Sport Psychology,* 5: 343–346.

Helfer, R. E., Kempe, C. H. (Eds.) (1976). *Child abuse and neglect: The family and the community.* Cambridge, MA: Ballinger.

Irby, D. M. (1986). Clinical teaching and the clinical teacher. *Journal of Medical Education,* 61 35–45.

Jason, H., Kagan, N., Werner, A., Elstein, A., & Thomas, J. B. (1971). New approaches to teaching basic interviewing skills to medical students. *American Journal of Psychiatry,* 127: 1404–1407.

Jason, H., & Westberg, J. (1982). *Teachers and teaching in U.S. medical schools*. Norwalk, CT: Appleton-Century-Crofts.

Johnson, D. W., & Maruyama, G. (1981). Effects of cooperative, competitive, and individualistic goal structures on achievement: A meta-analysis. *Psychological Bulletin*, 89(1): 47–62.

Kagan, N. (1978). Interpersonal process recall: Media in clinical and human interaction supervision. In M. M. Berger (Ed.), *Videotape techniques in psychiatric training and treatment* (2nd ed., pp. 70–84). New York: Brunner/Mazel.

Kagan, N. (1984a). Interpersonal process recall: Basic methods and recent research. In D. Larsen (Ed.) *Teaching psychological skills*. Monterey, CA: Brooks Cole.

Kagan, N. (1984b). The physician as therapeutic agent: Innovations in training. In C. Van Dyke, L. Temoshok, & L. S. Zegans (Eds.) *Emotions in health and illness: Applications to clinical practice*, pp. 209–226. New York: Grune and Stratton.

Kagan, N. & Kagan, H. (1991). Interpersonal process recall. In P. W. Dowrick (Ed.), *Practical guide to using video in the behavioral sciences*. (pp. 221–230). New York: John Wiley & Sons.

Kagan, N., & Krathwohl, D. R. (1967). *Studies in human interaction: Interpersonal process recall stimulated by videotape*. Research Report 20. East Lansing, MI: Michigan State University, Educational Publication Services.

Kahn, G. S., Cohen, B., & Jason, H. (1979a). Teaching interpersonal skills in family practice: results of a national survey. *Journal of Family Practice,* 8(2): 309–316.

Kahn, G. S., Cohen, B., & Jason, H. (1979b). The teaching of interpersonal skills in U.S. medical schools. *Journal of Medical Education*, 54: 29–35.

Kaufman, A. (Ed.) (1985). *Implementing problem-based medical education: Lessons from successful innovations*. New York: Springer Publishing Company.

Lewis, J. L., Stokes, D. R., Fischetti, L. R., & Rutledge, A. L. (1988). Using the patient as teacher: A training method for family practice residents in behavioral science. *Professional Psychology: Research and Practice*, 19: 349–352.

Lincoln R., Layton, J., & Holdman, H. (1978). Using simulated patients to teach assessment. *Nursing Outlook*, 26: 316–320.

Linn, B. S., Arostegni, M., & Zeppa, R. (1975). Performance rating scale for peer and self-assessment. *British Journal of Medical Education*, 9(2): 98–101.

Mao, C., Bullock, C. S., Harway, E. C., & Khalsa, S. K. (1988). A workshop on ethnic and cultural awareness for second-year students. *Journal of Medical Education*, 63: 624–628.

McCallum, J. (1987, April). Videotape is on a roll. *Sports Illustrated*, pp. 136–144.

McLeish, J., & Martin, J. (1975). Verbal behavior: a review and experimental analysis. *Journal of General Psychology,* 67: 198–203.

McNeese, M., & Hebeles, J. (1977). The abused child. Ciba, *Clinical Symposia*, 29: 5.

Morton, J. B., & Macbeth, W. A. A. G. (1977). Correlations between staff, peer and self-assessments of fourth-year students in surgery. *Medical Education,* 11: 167–170.

Novik, B. R. (1978). The effects of teaching interviewing skills and affective sensitivity to family medicine residents. Unpublished doctoral dissertation, Michigan State University, East Lansing.

Parrish J. M., & Babbitt, R. L. (1991). Video-mediated instruction in medical settings. In P.W. Dowrick (Ed.), *Practical guide to using video in the behavioral sciences.* (pp. 166–185). New York: John Wiley & Sons.

Personnel Journal. (1974). Conscious competency—the mark of a competent instructor. July: 538–539.

Reilly, D. E. (1958). *Nursing students' responses to the clinical field.* New York: Columbia University.

Resnikoff, A. (1968). The relationship of counselor behavior to client response and an analysis of medical interview training procedure involving simulated patients. Unpublished doctoral dissertation, Michigan State University.

Robbins, A. S., Kaus, D. R., Heinrich, R., Abrass, I., Dreye, J., & Clyman, B. (1979). Interpersonal skills: Evaluation in an internal medicine residency. *Journal of Medical Education*, 54: 885–894.

Robbins, A. S., Fink, A., Kosecoff, J., Vivell, S., & Beck, J. C. (1982). Studies in geriatric education: 2. Educational materials and programs. *Journal of the American Geriatrics Society*, 30: 340–347.

Ross, D., Bird, A. M., Doody, S. G., & Zoeller, M. (1985). Effects of modeling and videotape feedback with knowledge results on motor performance. *Human Movement Science*, 4: 149–157.

Rothstein, A. L. (1981, August). Using feedback to enhance learning and performance with emphasis on videotape replay. *Science Periodical on Research and Technology in Sport*, p. BU-1.

Rowe, M. B. (1986). Wait time: slowing down may be a way of speeding up. *Journal of Teacher Education*, 37: 43–50.

R. R. Bowker's Complete Video Directory. (1992). New Providence, NY: R. R. Bowker.

Schön, D.A. (1983). *The reflective practitioner: How professionals think in action*. New York: Basic Books.

Schön, D.A. (1987). *Educating the reflective practitioner: Toward a new design for teaching and learning in the professions.* San Francisco: Jossey-Bass.

Schön, D.A. (1991). *The reflective turn: Case studies in and on educational practice*. New York: Teachers College Press.

Schoonover, S. C., Bassuk, E. L., Smith, R., & Gaskill, D. (1983). The use of video programs to teach interpersonal skills. *Journal of Medical Education*, 58: 804–810.

Sharf, B. F., & Kahler, J. (1993) Furthermore. *Academic Medicine*, 68: 344–345.

Sparks, S. M., Vitalo, P. B., Cohen, B. F., & Kahn, G. S. (1980). Teaching of interpersonal skills to nurse practitioner students. *Journal of Continuing Education in Nursing*, 11(2): 7–16.

Spivack, J. S., & Kagan, N. (1972, September). Laboratory to classroom: The practical application of IPR in a masters level prepracticum counselor education program. *Counselor Education and Supervision*, pp. 3–15.

Stuart, M. R., Goldstein, H. S., & Snope, F. C. (1980). Self-evaluation by residents in family medicine. *Journal of Family Practice,* 10: 639–642.

Tannen, D. (1986). *That's not what I meant!: How conversational style makes or breaks relationships.* New York: William Morrow & Company.

Weiner, D. J. (Ed.). (1993). *The video source book*. 14th ed. Detroit: Gale Research.

Werner, A., & Schneider, J. M. (1974). Teaching medical students interactional skills: A research-based course in the doctor-patient relationship. *New England Journal of Medicine*, 290: 1232–1237.

Westberg, J., Kahn, G. S., Cohen, B., & Friel, T. (1980). Teaching interpersonal skills in physician assistant programs. *Medical Teacher*, 1: 136–141.

Westberg, J., & Jason H. (1987). *Communicating with patients* (video series of seven programs). Distributed by the Society of Teachers of Family Medicine, and Centre Communications, Boulder, CO.

Westberg, J., & Jason, H. (1989). *Clinical teaching* (video series of seven programs). Distributed by the Society of Teachers of Family Medicine, the American Journal of Nursing Company, and Centre Communications, Boulder, CO.

Westberg, J., & Jason, H. (1991). *Making presentations*. (Video tape), Distributed by the Society of Teachers of Family Medicine, the American Journal of Nursing Company, and Centre Communications, Boulder, CO.

Westberg, J., & Jason, H. (1993). *Collaborative clinical education: The foundation of effective patient care*, New York: Springer Publishing Company.

Whitman, N. A., & Schwenk, T. L. (1984). *Preceptors as teachers: A guide to clinical teaching*. Salt Lake City, UT: University of Utah.

Yura, H. & Walsh, M. (1983). *The nursing process* (4th ed.). New York: Appleton-Century-Crofts.

Author Index

Alexander, M., 13
Alfaro, R., 21
Arostegni, M., 142
Arnold, L., 142

Babbitt, R. L., 31
Barrows, H., 62, 99
Bassuk, E. L., 66
Bird, A. M., 31
Bolm, G., 138
Brookfield, S. D., 7
Bullock, C. S., 57

Calkins, E.V. 142
Chickering, A. W., 7
Cohen, B. 137
Cross, K. P., 4

DeGroot, A.D., 182
Dowrick, P. W., 31, 57, 67

Elstein, A. S., 21, 137
Ende, J., 164
Erffmeyer, E. S., 31

Feidel, D., 137
Fink, A., 57
Finley, B., 147
Foster, P. J., 75
Franks, I. M., 31, 142
Fuller, F., 147

Gagne, R. M., 5
Goldstein, H., S., 142

Hall, E. G., 31
Hall, M. N., 13
Hebeles, J., 164
Helfer, R. E., 164
Holdman, H., 35

Irby, D. M., 183

Jason, H., 11, 137, 144, 179
Jesdale, D. C., 31, 57, 67
Johnson, D. W., 181

Kagan, H., 55, 91, 138
Kagan, N., 55, 91, 137, 138
Kahler, J., 57
Kahn, G. S., 137
Kaufman, A., 62
Kaus, D. R., 57, 138
Kempe, C. H., 164
Kim, K., 147
Krathwohl, D. R., 91

Layton, J., 35
Lewis, J. L., 199
Lincoln, R., 35
Linn, B.S., 138

Macbeth, W. A. A. G., 142
Mao, C., 57
Maile, L. J., 31, 142
Manning, B. A., 147
Martin, J., 75
Maruyama, G., 181
McCallum, J., 91
McLeish, J., 75
McNeese, J., 164
Morton, J. B., 142
Mynatt, S., 147

Novik, B. R., 138

Parrish, J. M., 31
Pettice, Y. J., 13

Reilly, D. E., 156
Resnikoff, A., 138
Robbins, A. S., 57, 138
Ross, D., 31
Rothstein, A. L., 91
Rowe, M. B., 73

Schneider, J. M., 137
Schön, D. A., 140
Schoonover, S. C., 66
Schwenk, T. L., 38
Sharf, B. F., 57
Shulman, L.S., 21, 137
Snope, F., C., 142
Sparks, S. M., 137
Spivack, J. S., 137
Sprafka, S. A., 21, 137
Stokes, D. R., 199
Stuart, M. R., 142
Tamblyn, R., 62

Tannen, D., 173

Vitalo, P.B., 137

Walsh, M., 21
Werner, A., 137
Westberg, J., 11, 137, 144, 179
Weiner D. J., 13
Whitman, N. A., 38
Willoughby, T. L., 138

Yura, H., 21

Zeppa, R., 142

Subject Index

Active learning, *x*, *xii*, 3–11, 29, 104, 131
American Journal of Nursing Company, 64, 79
American Psychiatric Association, 64, 79
Assessment of learners' needs, 40–41, 99–100, 122, 186–189, 206
Attitudes and values, 59
Authoritarian model of health professions education, *xii*, 9–11, 148

Burns, Robert, 136

Centre Communications, 79
Classroom, as a theater, 25
teaching in, 4, 16, 25
CLE, *See* Clinical learning experience
Clients/Patients, *See* Patients/Clients
Clinical learning experience (CLE), *x*, 17
Clinical skills, *xii*
Clinical supervision, 17
Cognitive processes, 4
Collaborative model of health professions education, *xii*, 9–12, 181, 185
Competent, consciously and unconsciously, described, 38–39, 109, 161, 180
Conditions needed for lasting learning, 3, 5–9, 17–20
Consent forms, 119–120, *See also* Informed consent
Competition among learners, 11, 143, 181, 186, 190
Continuous quality improvement, 181
Copyright issues, 65, 68

Decision points in health care, 46–47, 91, 184, 139
Demonstrations, using video for, 18, **27–54**
  making video recordings of, 43–44
  reviewing recordings of, with learners, 44–48
Diagnostic posture/process, *See* Assessment of learners' needs
Discussions, fostering, with video triggers, 60, 68–78

Evaluation, summative, 110
Experts, limitations of, 39

Faculty development, video triggers for, 64

Feedback to learners, delivered in hurtful ways, 163–164
from peers, 10–11, 90–91, **179–198**,
from patients/clients, 90, 98–99, **199–217**,
from teachers, 4, 12, 19–20, 59, 133–134, 150, 154, **161–178**
from video recordings, 91, **133–160**,
general discussion, 8–9, 12
premature, 134, 150
Formats, videotape, 15, 66–67
Functionally grotesque, 85–86

Goals, learners', 10, 122, 141, 145–146, 149–150, 155, 169, 174 190–191, 209
teacher's goals for learner(s), 10, 68, 117, 141, 145, 149, 191, 209

Health Sciences Consortium, 64, 79
Home videos, 64

Illustrating events, with video, 27–30
Informed consent:
of learners, 114
of patients, 43, 113, 120, 204–205
Interpersonal processes skills, 4, 57–58, 61, 83–84, 202
Interpersonal process recall, 137–138
Interpersonal Process Recall Institute, 79
Invisible process of health care, 6, 12, 34, 46. *See also* Processes of health care

Journals, 156

Laboratory teaching, 28–29
Learner-centered education, 10–11
Learners:
active, independent, self-directed, (*See also* Active learning) 5–6, 10, 131, 148
defined, *xii*
dependent, passive, 11, 22, 148
lifelong, 9, 132
Learning goals, *See* Goals
Learning plans, 10

Michigan State University, 137
Modeling, **27–54**

National Institute of Health, 13, 106
National Library of Medicine, 13
Nonjudgemental approach, 74–75, 143–144, 152–153
Nonverbal behavior, 92, 138, 154

Observation of learners via video, rationale for, 20
Observational skills, 58
Open-ended approach, 143–144, 152–153
Ownership of learning, 6, 135

Patients/clients, defined, *xii*
as providers of feedback, 98–99
preparing them for videotaping and review session, **203–206**,
simulated, 19, 26, 39–40, 43, 83–84, 87–90, 123, 137, 146, 184, 199, 210
rationale for using, 40, 88–90
training of, 97–99
standardized, 90, *See also* Patients/clients, Simulated

Peer review, **179–198**
Peer teaching, 179
Practice of skills, (systematic, sequenced, supervised), 4, 6, 19, 48, 57–58, **85–88**
Problem-based learning, 62–64
Processes of health care, *x*, 4, 6, 21,
Processes of learning, 21
Processes, invisible (internal) and visible, 6, 18, 34, 46, 91–92
Process skills, 12

Reflective, helping learners to be, 7, 34, 92, 131–160, 181–182, 188
Reviewing recordings of demonstrations, reasons for, 33–35
Risk taking, 85–86
Role model, teacher as, 6, 18, 30–31,144–145, 192
Role playing, 78, **83–108**
  further readings, 106
  preparing learners for, 99–103
  scripts for, 94–95

Self-assessment and self-critique by learners, 7, 10, 19, **131–160**, 184
Simulation, 19, 26, 39–40, 43, **83–101**, 123, 137, 146, 184, 210
Simulated patients/clients, *See* Patients/clients, simulated
Skills, practice of, *See* Practice of skills
Society for Teachers of Family Medicine, 64, 79

Teacher-centered education, 10–11
Trust, among learners, 9, 20, 185–6
  between learners and teachers, 9, 20, 114, 135, 147–8, 168, 186
  between patients and learners, 114, 207, 212

Video clips, 13–14, 35–36, **55–82**
Video equipment, 15–16, 22, 117–118
  needed for making and reviewing role plays, 95
  permanently installed in clinical settings, 115
Video formats, 15, 66–67
Video log, 19, 155
Video-modeling, 31
Video playback, multiple times, 34
Video triggers, 14, 22, **55–82**, *See also* Video clips
  from home videos, 65–66
  from off-air TV programs, 65
  from motion pictures, 65
  from recordings made by learners and teachers, 65–66
Video recordings, how to make:
  further readings, 128
  general, **111–130**
  of your interviews, 48–51
  of role-played events, 94–96
Video resources, 12–14
Video standards, international, 67
Video viewing distance, 15
Vignettes, 14, 55, *See also*, Video triggers, Video clips

Wait time, 73–74, 76